Interpreting American History:

The Age of Andrew Jackson

INTERPRETING AMERICAN HISTORY SERIES

Brian D. McKnight and James S. Humphreys, series editors

THE AGE OF ANDREW JACKSON
Edited by Brian D. McKnight and James S. Humphreys

INTERPRETING AMERICAN HISTORY

The Age of
ANDREW JACKSON

Edited by

BRIAN D. MCKNIGHT

and

JAMES S. HUMPHREYS

The Kent State University Press

Kent, Ohio

© 2011 by The Kent State University Press, Kent, Ohio 44242

ALL RIGHTS RESERVED
Library of Congress Catalog Card Number 2011000682
ISBN 978-1-60635-098-0
Manufactured in the United States of America

LIBRARY OF CONGRESS CATALOGING-IN-PUBLICATION DATA
Interpreting American history. The age of Andrew Jackson / edited by
Brian D. McKnight and James S. Humphreys.
    p. cm. — (Interpreting American history series)
  Includes bibliographical references and index.
  ISBN 978-1-60635-098-0 (pbk. : alk. paper) ∞
  1. United States—Politics and government—1829-1837—Historiography. 2.
Jackson, Andrew, 1767-1845—Historiography. I. McKnight, Brian Dallas.
II. Humphreys, James Scott, 1963- III. Title: Age of Andrew Jackson.
  E381.I58 2011
  973.5′6 092—dc22

                        2011000682

British Library Cataloging-in-Publication data are available.

15 14 13 12 11   5 4 3 2 1

Contents

Foreword

Interpreting American History Series

Of all the history courses taught on college campuses, historiography is one of the most challenging. The historiographic essays most often available are frequently too specialized for broad teaching and sometimes too rigorous for the average undergraduate student. Every day, frustrated scholars and students search for writings that offer both breadth and depth in their approach to the historiography of different eras and movements. As young scholars grow more intellectually mature, they search for literature, sometimes in vain, that will clarify historiographical points. As graduate students prepare for seminar presentations, comprehensive examinations, and dissertation work, they continue to search for works that will help to place their work within the broader study. Then, when they complete their studies and enter the professoriat, they find themselves less intellectually connected to the ideas that they once showed a mastery of, and they again ask about the lack of meaningful and succinct studies of historiography . . . and the circle continues.

Within the pages of this series, innovative young scholars discuss the different interpretations of the important eras and events of history, focusing not only on the intellectual shifts that have taken place but also on the various catalysts that drove these shifts. It is the hope of the series editors that these volumes fill the aforementioned intellectual voids and speak to young scholars in a way that will supplement their other learning, that the same pages that speak to undergraduate students will also remind the established scholar of his or her historiographic roots, that a difficult subject will be made more accessible to curious minds, and that these ideas are not lost among the details offered within the classroom.

BRIAN D. MCKNIGHT, University of Virginia's College at Wise
JAMES S. HUMPHREYS, Murray State University

Introduction

"History will be kind to me," British prime minister Winston Churchill reportedly declared, "for I intend to write it."[1] Churchill's remark demonstrates that he understood the enormous power historians possess in shaping how history is viewed by both their generation and those who come after them. Like Churchill, scholars feel a burden to illuminate the meaning of the past. To meet this challenge, they ply their craft with care and precision, hoping to develop the most accurate view of history possible, and their efforts often result in new interpretations that may contradict ideas put forth by earlier historians. Rarely, however, do they fulfill the goal of creating new historical paradigms without a challenge from other scholars. Because historians often vociferously disagree among themselves over the causes and meanings of past events, creating a cacophony of interpretations, controversy seems to follow them. These realities concerning the quest for historical accuracy make this volume of historiographical essays extremely useful to students, scholars, and general readers seeking to learn how truth, or at least an approximation of it, emerges from the clash of interpretations that always attends the study of history.

The essays in this volume address the changing views of scholars over the past century about a watershed era in United States history: the age of Andrew Jackson. Rough-hewn frontiersman, Indian fighter, hero of the Battle of New Orleans, and two-term president of the United States, Jackson became a "symbol for an age," as John William Ward wrote in 1955.[2] There was plenty of substance behind that symbol. Constant hardship bedeviled Jackson. The death of his mother during the American Revolution, the suffering brought on by innumerable injuries and illnesses, the ignominy of having killed an opponent in a duel, and the death of his beloved wife, Rachel, soon after his election to the presidency in 1828 all tested his resolve and might have reduced a lesser man to cynicism and despair. Jackson showed a virtually inhuman will to succeed as he persevered through these trials. Jackson, however, was human—all too human, as his bad temper, violent nature, and overbearing manner clearly demonstrated. Little wonder, then, that the complexities of Jackson's personal and public life have engendered a myriad of conflicting interpretations of Old Hickory's era and his legacy.

The Age of Jackson was not unlike many later times. Jackson stands out among early presidents as the first activist chief executive, shaping policy himself instead of deferring to the wishes of Congress and intimidating rather than placating his opponents. Long before the development of the "imperial presidency" in the twentieth century, Jackson's actions seemed, in the estimation of his critics, dangerously close to those of a dictator.[3] Rather than playing the role of the American king, as his adversaries in the Whig Party accused him of doing, Jackson instead proved to be a powerful leader who widened constitutional boundaries on the presidency without destroying them. He always strove to serve what he considered the best interests of the United States, or more accurately the best interests of white America, although today a number of his policies, especially Indian removal, seem morally indefensible. The robust manner in which Jackson wielded presidential authority set a precedent for future presidents, most notably Abraham Lincoln and Franklin Roosevelt, who felt compelled to assume extraordinary powers during times of national emergencies. Clearly, then, if history holds lessons for the present, Americans can learn a great deal by studying the Age of Jackson. They are fortunate to have such able guides—Richard Hofstadter, Arthur M. Schlesinger, Charles Sellers, Robert V. Remini, and other renowned historians who have written about Old Hickory—to direct them through the thickets of Jacksonian America.

Just as these historians analyzed the issues of Jackson's day, the seven scholars who have contributed chapters to this volume analyze the work of these historians. With great skill and precision, the essayists bring order and understanding to the large corpus of writing related to Jacksonian America. Mark R. Cheathem's opening chapter explains where the major works written about Jackson fit into the larger currents of American historiography from 1850 to the present. Cheathem recently published a biography of Andrew Jackson Donelson, the nephew of Andrew Jackson, in which he portrays Donelson as a disappointing politician who never fulfilled the hopes his famous uncle placed in him.[4] Cheathem's chapter provides a context for understanding the other six writings that follow. Kristofer Ray, author of an excellent study of the development of popular democracy in middle Tennessee in the late eighteenth and early nineteenth centuries, analyzes the historiography of the "corrupt bargain," an alleged scandal that Jackson partisans believed led unfairly to Old Hickory's defeat in the election of 1824.[5] The corrupt bargain, however, provided Jackson's forces with a cause célèbre in the presidential election four years later. Wade Shaffer examines the historiography of Jacksonian politics, which prompted the emergence of a second party system in antebellum America. Kevin M. Gannon explores the scholarly arguments surrounding Jackson's role in resolving the standoff between South Carolina lawmakers and federal officials during the nullification crises of the early 1830s. John T. Ellisor delves into the historiography of Indian removal, which Jackson sought and executed with shocking vigor.[6] Historians' views toward the social issues of Jackson's day receive scrutiny from Beth A. Salerno, and Ryan Ruckel examines what historians have said about economic developments engendered by the market revolution in Jacksonian America. These incisive chapters, written by expert scholars, should not only acquaint readers with the nineteenth-century world of Andrew Jackson and the ways in which historians have interpreted Old Hickory's life and times but also enable them to better understand the world in which they live. After all, any legitimate historical inquiry recognizes the role historians play in interpreting the crucial link between the present and the past.

Notes

1. "Quotations by Author: Sir Winston Churchill (1874-1965)," Quotations Page, www.quotationspage.com.

2. John William Ward, *Andrew Jackson: Symbol for an Age* (New York: Oxford Univ. Press, 1955).

3. Arthur M. Schlesinger, *The Imperial Presidency* (Boston: Houghton Mifflin, 1973).

4. Mark R. Cheathem, *Old Hickory's Nephew: The Political and Private Struggles of Andrew Jackson Donelson* (Baton Rouge: Louisiana State Univ. Press, 2007).

5. Kristofer Ray, *Middle Tennessee, 1775-1825: Progress and Popular Democracy on the Southwestern Frontier* (Knoxville: Univ. of Tennessee Press, 2007).

6. John T. Ellisor, *The Second Creek War: Interethnic Conflict and Collusion on a Collapsing Frontier,* Indians of the Southeast Series (Lincoln: Univ. of Nebraska Press, 2010).

CHAPTER ONE

"The Shape of Democracy"

Historical Interpretations of Jacksonian Democracy

MARK R. CHEATHEM

Alexis de Tocqueville, that renowned observer of American society during the 1830s, wrote that when he visited the United States, "I saw in America more than America; it was the shape of democracy itself which I sought, its inclination, character, prejudices, and passions; I wanted to understand it so as at least to know what we have to fear or hope therefrom." For decades, students and scholars agreed with Tocqueville, looking to the Jacksonian period to find the origins of modern conceptions of equality and democracy. In recent years, however, the study of Jacksonian America has fallen victim to the period's failure to realize fully the nation's promise of those political and social ideals. But as one historian has noted, "that very standard by which historians judge and often condemn Jacksonian America is itself a legacy of Jacksonian America." Examining the development of the United States in the years between its second war for independence from Great Britain and the Civil War seems a worthy endeavor for many reasons, not the least of which are pursuing Tocqueville's goal of understanding "the shape of democracy" and ascertaining how Americans of the Jacksonian period established a legacy by which they could be judged.[1]

The Patrician (or Whig) School—1850s-1890s

The first scholarly study of the Jacksonian period appeared as the nation entered the Civil War. James Parton's three-volume *Life of Andrew Jackson* offered a comprehensive assessment of Jackson's personal and private life. He was, Parton wrote, "a man whose ignorance, whose good intentions, and whose passions combined to render him, of all conceivable human beings, the most unfit for the office." Parton also found Jackson full of contradictions: he was at once "a democratic autocrat. An urbane savage. An atrocious saint." Parton's paradoxical assessment of the seventh president, as one historian noted in 1958, "could almost stand today as the conclusion to a review of Jacksonian historiography."[2]

Other historians of the mid-to-late nineteenth century also found Jackson lacking. William Graham Sumner called him "a 'barbarian' who 'acted from spite, pique, instinct, prejudice or emotion.'" Hermann E. Von Holst labeled Jackson an "'arrogant general' whose 'mind was as untrained as his passions were unbridled.'" Not only did these scholars find Jackson's personality and intellect wanting, but they also decried his democratization of American politics. "'Since Jackson,' von Holst argued, 'the people have begun to exchange the leadership of a small number of statesmen and politicians of a higher order for the rule of an ever increasing crowd of politicians of high and low degree, down even to the pothouse politician and the common thief, in the protecting mantle of demagogism.'" Moisei Ostrogorski lamented that Jacksonian democracy "'excluded men of sterling worth and high principles from public life.'"[3]

The venom with which these scholars denounced Jackson and his effect on American politics appear less surprising when one recognizes their socioeconomic background. They all were part of the patrician class, the well-off and well-educated East Coast elite that had provided the early leadership for the United States. It was their segment of society that had found itself on the losing end of the Jacksonian political revolution, as Old Hickory's alliance implemented the infamous "spoils system" that supposedly threw the patrician class out of office, replacing them with the "common man." Despite agreeing with some of Jackson's policies, such as his opposition to the Second Bank of the United States and the South Carolina nullifiers, the patrician school of historians' acerbic criticisms stood out as an indictment of Jacksonian democracy.[4]

THE PROGRESSIVE (OR AGRARIAN-DEMOCRATIC) SCHOOL—1890S-1940S

The 1890s witnessed a shift in the scholarly interpretation of Jacksonian democracy; the work of Frederick Jackson Turner was seminal in this transition. Turner saw Jackson as the logical outcome of the democratizing influence of the American frontier: "Out of this frontier democratic society where the freedom and abundance of land in the great Valley opened a refuge to the oppressed in all regions, came the Jacksonian democracy which governed the nation after the downfall of the party of John Quincy Adams." In contrast to the patrician historians, Turner was convinced that "Jacksonian Democracy . . . [was] strong in the faith of the intrinsic excellence of the common man, in his right to make his own place in the world, and in his capacity to share in government."[5]

Turner served as the leader of the emerging Progressive school of history. Much like their political counterparts, the Progressive historians were largely middle class, with many native to rural areas and small towns in the South, the Midwest, and the West. These socioeconomic and geographical differences from the patrician historians provided a different perspective on the political battles of the Jacksonian period. Progressive historians tended to see them as a series of sectional conflicts among the West, the South, and the East that brought the nation closer to the democratic ideal as westerners and southerners overthrew the elitist eastern political hegemony. As Turner described the conflicts, "Inevitable in such a changing country were sectional interests, sectional antagonisms, and sectional combinations. Each great area was evolving in its own way. Each had its own type of people, its own geographic and economic basis, its own particular economic and social interests."[6]

Though he set the Progressive agenda, Turner was not the only adherent, of course. William E. Dodd presented Jackson "'as a second Jefferson.'" John Spencer Bassett's biography of Jackson praised him for "his brave, frank, masterly leadership of the democratic movement.... Few American Presidents have better lived up to the demands of the movement which brought them into power." Even John Fiske, a disciple of the social Darwinist views of Herbert Spencer, conceded the positive effects of Jackson's presidency. The Tennessean "had checked 'a tendency toward the mollycoddling, old granny theory of government, according to which the ruling powers are to take care of the people, build their roads for them, do their banking for them, rob Peter to pay Paul for carrying on a losing business, and tinker and bemuddle things generally.'"[7]

Even when historians disagreed with the Progressive view, they still made their arguments in the arena created by Turner. Two of Jackson's fiercest critics, Thomas P. Abernethy and Richard Stenberg, focused on the sectional divide as they attacked what they perceived as the myth of Jacksonian egalitarianism. Abernethy's *From Frontier to Plantation in Tennessee* presented Jackson "as a frontier nabob who took sides against the democratic movement in his own state." In criticizing what he deemed Jackson's paradoxical support of both states' rights and nationalism, Abernethy wrote, "Not only was Jackson not a consistent politician, he was not even a real leader of democracy.... Jackson never really championed the cause of the people; he only invited them to champion his." Stenberg excoriated Jackson in a series of articles, many of which centered on his involvement in territorial expansion in Florida and Texas. Stenberg was convinced that Jackson illegally invaded Spanish Florida and both destroyed and created evidence to cover up his disingenuousness on that account. He also believed that Jackson was behind Sam Houston's abandonment of the Tennessee governorship and his role in the Texas revolution a few years later.[8]

THE URBAN SCHOOL—1940S-1950S

The Turnerian vision of Jacksonian democracy was challenged in 1945 by the publication of Arthur M. Schlesinger Jr.'s *The Age of Jackson.* In many ways, *The Age of Jackson* served as both the apex of the Progressive interpretation and the foundation of new interpretations focused on urban cities in the East that argued over the question of whether the Jacksonian movement opposed capitalistic excesses or sought to open capitalism to all classes. Schlesinger viewed the Jacksonian period "as a problem not of sections but of classes." Instead of locating the nexus of Jacksonian democracy along the western frontier, Schlesinger believed that the eastern urban working classes were the impetus for Jacksonian reform. It was the urban laborers who strived for economic egalitarianism through their attempts to limit exploitation by business interests. For him, "the essential meaning of the Jacksonian upheaval [was] in its economic, rather than in its political, objectives." Just as many scholars viewed Franklin D. Roosevelt's presidency as the culmination of the Populist and Progressive movements of the late nineteenth and early twentieth centuries, Schlesinger saw Jacksonian democracy as the result of a combined urban-rural coalition that gave rise to liberal reform.[9]

The Schlesinger thesis precipitated a spate of new studies that challenged his argument that the urban working classes propelled Jacksonian reform. In surveying the economic battles of the period, these historians emphasized the entrepreneurial, capitalistic spirit of the Jacksonians. Bray Hammond believed that Jackson destroyed the Second Bank of the United States because it threatened economic opportunity for middle-class businessmen. In reviewing Schlesinger's book, Hammond declared, "It represents the age of Jackson as one of triumphant liberalism when it was as much or more an age of triumphant exploitation." Richard Hofstadter "saw in Jackson a president who was fundamentally probusiness" and supportive of "the ambitions of the small capitalist." Joseph Dorfman argued that entrepreneurial businessmen, not the workers themselves, led the charge for labor reform. Richard B. Morris and two of his students, William A. Sullivan and Edward Pessen, found little support for Jackson among the urban working classes and little sympathy by Jackson for urban laborers. Walter Hugins proposed that the labor movement in New York was supported by a cross section of individuals from varied socioeconomic backgrounds who were intent on "further[ing] the democratization of this capitalist society" in order to minimize the elite class's economic power.[10]

THE ETHNOCULTURAL SCHOOL—1960S-1970S

The most significant challenge to the Schlesinger thesis appeared in 1961 with the publication of Lee Benson's *The Concept of Jacksonian Democracy: New York as a Test Case.* In his examination of party politics in New York, Benson used quantitative voting data to conclude that ethnic and religious differences, not class and economic differences, among voters defined the struggle between Democrats and Whigs. His "ethnocultural" approach supported the consensus school's interpretation of U.S. history, which "allowed for conflict over 'status' questions," while at the same time "[denying] the centrality of class in a society unified by a 'fiercely individualistic and capitalistic' political culture."[11]

Benson's argument and methods marked an important transition in Jacksonian historiographical debates. While usually not supportive of the consensus interpretation, studies throughout the 1960s and 1970s often took Benson's study as a starting point to uncover how significant ethnocultural differences were to Jacksonian politics. Historians tended to give more attention to local and state politics rather than the usual focus on national parties and leaders. Alternative ways of approaching history, such as the use of quantitative methodology and psychohistorical analysis, also appeared as part of the ethnocultural approach.

Some historians, in particular Ronald P. Formisano and Paul Kleppner, reinforced Benson's ethnocultural thesis. Formisano's study of Michigan downplayed the connection between national and local politics. National politics was, in his view, the province of an elite few and focused on the great issues of the day, such as nullification and the Bank War. Local politics, meanwhile, was the concern of the masses and centered on topics related to ethnicity and morality, such as immigration and temperance. Kleppner's study of the mid-to-late nineteenth-century American electoral system, which included the end of the Jacksonian period, explicitly argued that the political parties of the era were "coalitions of social groups sharing similar ethnocultural values."[12]

In a 1960 article and a book published in 1966, Richard P. McCormick debunked the commonly held claim that Jackson's election reflected, in Frederick A. Ogg's words, a "mighty democratic uprising." His analysis of voting data revealed that not until after Jackson left office did American voters become enthusiastic about political participation; thus, Jackson's political agenda was not the impetus of democratization, as previous historians had argued. One of the most scathing critiques of the Jacksonian era's political parties was Edward Pessen's *Jacksonian America: Society, Personality, and Politics.* Pessen found that "the men elected to office in antebellum elections," regardless of the office, party affiliation, or regional identity, "were with few exceptions inordinately well-to-do and of high prestige occupation, rather than small farmers, clerks, and workingmen. For all the differences in their political rhetoric, the major parties of the era were more like than unlike."[13]

One interesting result of the evolution of ethnocultural scholarship during the 1960s and 1970s was the application of psychological theory to past events, of which the Jacksonian period offered substantial material for analysis. Marvin Meyers's *The Jacksonian Persuasion* was a seminal work in that regard. Meyers argued that "Jacksonians blamed the Bank [the Second Bank of the United States] for the transgressions committed by the people of their era against the political, social, and economic values of the Old Republic." By targeting the bank, they laid out a formula for success: "death to the Monster; life and health to the old republican values." In essence, Americans were experiencing a crisis of status anxiety, which led them to identify a scapegoat on which to place their fears.[14]

Andrew Jackson also became the subject of psychological analysis. Michael Paul Rogin's *Fathers and Children* attempted to explain Jackson's actions as an adult by "[employing] psychoanalysis to interpret cultural symbols." Rogin suggested that "when enemies challenged Jackson's reputation, they spoke the language of his inner accusers," which existed because Jackson had never known his father. Jackson and other white politicians pursued the dispossession of, and practiced paternalism toward, Native Americans "to regain the primal infant-mother connection from a position of domination instead of dependence." The result was a schizophrenic nation split between "benevolence and greed, power and helplessness." James C. Curtis, in *Andrew Jackson and the Search for Vindication,* found in his analysis of Jackson, who was the product of a chaotic frontier community, a man "consumed with anger and guilt" over his mother's death during the American Revolution. Unable to blame his mother for sacrificing herself for her relatives, yet in doing so leaving him an orphan, Jackson projected his anger at being left alone "outward onto someone, something. There were always acceptable scapegoats: the Indians, the British, the Bank." Curtis echoed Rogin's argument, concluding that "Indians represented disorder, a threat to white family solidarity and community stability, the lack of which contributed to Jackson's own wildness, anger, and insecurity. . . . Jackson feared and hated the Indian, but in a sense he needed him, too."[15]

THE IDEOLOGICAL SCHOOL—1970S-1980S

As the ethnocultural interpretation continued to influence Jacksonian scholarship, some historians reexamined the importance of the period's ideological origins and expressions. In the mid-1950s, John William Ward had assayed a significant ideological interpretation in *Andrew Jackson: Symbol for an Age.* He emphasized that "'Nature,' 'Providence,' and 'Will'" served as "the structural underpinnings of the ideology of the society of early nineteenth-century America, for which Andrew Jackson is one symbol." Ward unraveled a Jacksonian ideology comprising nineteenth-century Americans' practical and spiritual ties to the land, their belief in Manifest Destiny, and their confidence in self-determination. This interpretation harkened back to Turner's frontier thesis; later ideological studies were more complex in explaining Jacksonian and Whig political ideology.[16]

Classical republicanism was the organizing ideological concept that many historians of the United States, including those studying the Jacksonian period, embraced in the 1970s. Classical republicanism as a historical interpretation emerged largely with the publication of three major works in the late 1960s and early 1970s: Bernard Bailyn, *The Ideological Origins of the American Revolution;* Gordon S. Wood, *The Creation of the American Republic, 1776-1787;* and J. G. A. Pocock, *The Machiavellian Moment: Florentine Political Thought and the Atlantic Republican Tradition.* Historians identified classical republicanism with the ideology of the Opposition Whigs of eighteenth-century Britain; its general components included the fear of political corruption, the maintenance of a virtuous citizenry, and the establishment and preservation of a republican form of government. In the republican system of the United States, they argued, virtue (private moral conduct and self-sacrifice for the good of the community) and popular sovereignty (the expression of the people's will in a federal government) were two of the basic principles. The political battles of the Jacksonian period, then, were simply a continuation of the contested definitions of these eighteenth-century concepts.[17]

In a masterful three-volume biography of Jackson, as well as in biographies of Henry Clay and Daniel Webster and studies of the Bank War and Indian removal, Robert V. Remini appealed to classical republicanism as central to understanding the evolution and emergence of Jacksonian democracy. Influenced early on by conservative Jeffersonian Republicans, he argued, Jackson believed in limited government, the will of the people, and the dangers of national debt and consolidated national authority. Remini replaced John William Ward's three concepts of nature, providence, and will with a three-point conceptual framework of his own: empire, freedom, and democracy. "From the time he arrived in Tennessee," Remini argued, "Jackson absorbed powerful sentiments against all barriers to westward expansion and economic prosperity." Jackson imbibed "a narrow interpretation of the federal Constitution . . . one that reflected western concern for the rights and sovereignty of the states." John H. Eaton's *The Letters of Wyoming* "provided a blueprint of the ideological intentions of the developing Jacksonian movement. It was a statement of what Jackson's drive for the presidency was all about." His "political thought was a throwback to the Revolution and its most democratic ideals," Remini concluded. Jackson's Nullification Proclamation was his "unique contribution to a more profound understanding and appreciation of the American experiment in democracy and constitutional government. He was the first American statesman to offer the doctrine of the Union as a perpetual entity."[18]

Other studies echoed the classical republican interpretation. William J. Cooper's *The South and the Politics of Slavery, 1828-1856* emphasized the unity of antebellum white southerners against attacks on slavery. "In its political form," he wrote, "slavery became the cherished, visible symbol of independence, honor, and equality precisely because it embraced the most fundamental values of southern white society held in common by slaveowner and non-slaveowner alike." Both Whigs and Democrats "paid equal homage to the same sovereign—the people or the voters," while arguing that the opposing party was the true threat to liberty. J. Mills Thornton III's study of Alabama and Harry L. Watson's study of Cumberland County, North Carolina, reinforced the assertion that southern politicians galvanized white voters by appealing to a unity born out of fear that someone (e.g., Jackson, Henry Clay, Hugh Lawson White), some group (e.g., Whigs, Democrats, abolitionists), or some entity (e.g., the Second Bank of the United States) was seeking to subvert their liberty through an unconstitutional accumulation of power. Richard B. Latner's work on Jackson's presidency and his advisors also emphasized the Tennessean's "Jeffersonianism." Highlighting the influence of westerners such as Amos Kendall and Francis P. Blair on Jackson's administrations, Latner concluded that Jackson's ideology, which was "basically Jeffersonian in origin," upheld the idea "that while a republic must be strong enough to maintain unity and independence, its moral fiber must remain unblemished by extravagance, aristocratic pretension, and special interest legislation."[19]

Classical republicanism was not wholly the purview of histories focused on southerners and westerners, however. In *Chants Democratic: New York City and the Rise of the American Working Class, 1788-1850,* Sean Wilentz uncovered the symbols and rhetoric of republicanism among workingmen's parties in the Jacksonian period. "Faced with profound changes in the social relations of production," he wrote, "ordinary New Yorkers began to reinterpret their shared ideals of commonwealth, virtue, independence, citizenship, and equality, and struggled over the very meaning of the terms." As American social and economic relations changed, "masters and journeymen in the dividing crafts began to invent opposing interpretations of the artisan republican legacy." What developed among artisans was what Wilentz termed "classical republican trade unionism." Born out of the Bank War, this new class consciousness suggested that "resistance to capital, defense of the Republic, and preservation of their rights to associate and to set the price of their labor were one and the same cause."[20]

The publication of Harry L. Watson's *Liberty and Power: The Politics of Jacksonian America* offered both a masterful synthesis of the ideological school and an indication of where Jacksonian scholarship was headed. Watson argued for the primacy of classical republican ideology and rhetoric, particularly in defining the concepts of "liberty" and "power." Liberty had many meanings to Jacksonian-era Americans, but at its political core it referred to the majority rule of whites and the guarantee of the freedoms articulated in the Constitution. It also held other implications, including the necessity of individual and community self-control in order to protect minority rights. Liberty was threatened by power; as Watson nicely summarized the difference, "if liberty was the promise of self-control in self-governing communities, power was the threat of control by others." These republican concepts, as well as others such as virtue and morality, began to change during the Jacksonian period as "social and economic change put strains on the older political framework that it could not accommodate." Watson concluded that the introduction of the two-party political system, which largely centered on whether one liked Jackson and his policies, allowed Americans to debate these changes through an organized party structure and a shared ideological language.[21]

THE MARKET REVOLUTION SCHOOL—1990S

In his *Liberty and Power,* Watson alluded to the growing importance of a market revolution to Jacksonian historiography. A 1982 article by Sean Wilentz also proposed that Jacksonian historians needed to turn their attention to the market revolution, "with an even greater emphasis on changing social relations and popular ideology." The market revolution to which Watson and Wilentz-referred, as one historian defined it, was "a largely subsistence economy of small farms and tiny workshops, satisfying mostly local needs through barter and exchange, [which] gave place to an economy in which farmers and manufacturers produced food and goods for the cash rewards of an often distant marketplace." The changes wrought by the market revolution affected many parts of American society, including transportation (the modernization of roads and the development of canals, the railroad, and the steamboat), communication (faster transit time because of advancements in transportation, as well as the development of the telegraph), industrialization (the growth of the factory system), and the social relationships of spouses, families, workers, and slaves.[22]

Charles Sellers's *The Market Revolution: Jacksonian America, 1815–1846* attempted to address in comprehensive fashion the effects of the market revolution. Following the War of 1812, he argued, "history's most revolutionary force, the capitalist market, was wresting the American future from history's most conservative force, the land." Jacksonians opposed the encroachment of the market revolution, which produced "feelings of insecurity and powerlessness," while Whigs focused on expanding and supporting the market revolution. The political lesson of the period, according to Sellers, was that "democracy was born in tension with capitalism, and not as its natural and legitimizing political expression." Politics was only part of Sellers's survey of the period; his synthesis touched on nearly every aspect of American society, from the end of the War of 1812 through the conclusion of the Mexican-American War. As one reviewer noted, he "set the story in terms of essential dichotomies: states' rights/nationalism; antinomianism/arminianism; God/Mammon."[23]

Sellers's *The Market Revolution* elicited wide-ranging explorations and applications of the interpretative framework to various aspects of the Jacksonian era. One particularly important collection of essays, *The Market Revolution in America: Social, Political, and Religious Expressions, 1800-1880,* offered myriad uses of the market revolution thesis. Christopher Clark and Harry Watson looked at its effects on both the North and South. Amy Dru Stanley analyzed the marketplace in relation to the family. The market revolution's influence on political ideology concerned Eric Foner and John Ashworth, while Richard E. Ellis, Donald Ratcliffe, Sean Wilentz, and Michael Holt examined its shaping of Jacksonian politics. Daniel Walker Howe and Richard Carwardine addressed religion and the marketplace. Charles Sellers concluded with an appraisal of the essays in the book and engaged some of their criticisms. A similar forum took place in a special issue of the *Journal of the Early Republic,* in which Richard E. Ellis, Mary H. Blewett, Joel H. Silbey, Major L. Wilson, Harry L. Watson, and Amy Bridges critiqued *The Market Revolution,* with Sellers giving his response.[24]

Over the next several years, Sellers's work set the interpretive agenda for Jacksonian historians. Donald B. Cole's examination of Jackson's presidency, for instance, argued that "whatever policies Jackson followed, he was powerless to hold back the market revolution." While not explicitly crediting Sellers for his influence, Anne C. Rose's *Voices of the Marketplace* explored the antebellum period through the "systems of values" of Christianity, democracy, and capitalism, arguing that "the exchange of goods and ideas

[w]as the most distinctive development of the antebellum period." One historian, Daniel Feller, refused to use the term *market revolution* in the text of his synthetic treatment of the Jacksonian period. His introduction, however, acknowledged Sellers's thesis, and one cannot help but read Feller's presentation of an optimistic United States as a response to the "uncertainty and insecurity" that permeated Sellers's interpretation.[25]

Feller, in particular, was critical of the market revolution thesis, suggesting that it was "already ossifying from a lively idea to a deadening dogma," but others found it lacking as well. Christopher Clark questioned the inevitability of "the cultural outcomes of the changes" attributed to the marketplace and the market revolution. He warned that as the two terms "change[d] imperceptibly from descriptive categories of activities to reified explanatory forces," they came close to becoming "an abstract, catch-all explanation, resistant to detailed examination." William Shade highlighted Sellers's lack of attention to Jackson's proslavery and pro-Native American removal policies, while Edward Pessen criticized his study as suffering from "strained and at times perverse readings of events, which are too often communicated in opaque prose."[26]

By the turn of the millennium, the market revolution thesis appeared to have lost its currency as the latest explanation of the Jacksonian period. In fact, the period itself seemed to have become less important. It had, according to one scholar, "become something of a dead zone between the founding era and the Civil War."[27]

RECENT WORKS: HAS A NEW SYNTHESIS EMERGED?

Despite warnings that the Jacksonian period was losing its influence, recent years have witnessed a resurgence of interest in both Jackson the man and the period associated with him. Several new biographies appeared, as did two attempts to synthesize the period: one focused on the development of democracy; the other centered on the communications revolution.

For nearly two decades, Robert Remini's three-volume biography seemingly dissuaded other historians from tackling Old Hickory in biographical form, but several new biographies of Andrew Jackson have appeared in recent years. Hendrik Booraem's *Young Hickory: The Making of Andrew Jackson* attempted to explain Jackson by examining his Scotch-Irish origins and his early life. While too speculative at times, Booraem made an important contribution by reminding scholars that "Jackson at twenty-one was essentially the same person he would be for the rest of his life. Tennessee would be the theater of his exploits, but it did nothing to shape his personality." Andrew Burstein's *The Passions of Andrew Jackson* presented a study of Jackson's "passions" through his friendships with a handful of men, including Sam Houston and John Eaton. While containing some interesting insights into Jackson's behavior, Burstein's study was unsatisfying and contradictory, failing to offer much clarity about what actually drove the Tennessean's actions. Although well written, H. W. Brands's *Andrew Jackson: His Life and Times,* published in 2005, was a disappointing biography from a scholarly perspective, relying too heavily at times on unreliable sources, specifically Augustus C. Buell's *History of Andrew Jackson,* to make significant arguments about Jackson. The same year witnessed the publication of Sean Wilentz's biographical sketch of Jackson. He believed that Jackson was "best understood . . . as both a product of the American Revolution and a shaper of the larger Age of the Democratic Revolution in which he lived. . . . [H]e was, in many respects, a transitional figure in the history of American democratic politics."[28]

Wilentz built on this assessment of Jackson in his synthetic *The Rise of American Democracy: Jefferson to Lincoln.* Explaining the development of democracy ("a troublesome word") was his focus. He argued that Jacksonian historians since Arthur M. Schlesinger Jr., from whose *Age of Jackson* Wilentz's interpretation owes much, had "generally submerged the history of politics in the history of social change, reducing politics and democracy to by-products of various social forces without quite allowing the play of politics its importance." Wilentz made clear his disagreement with historians such as Charles Sellers: "Americans perceived" social change "primarily in political terms. . . . [P]olitics, government, and constitutional order, not economics, were primary to interpreting the world and who ran it."[29]

One preeminent scholar in particular found Wilentz's interpretive explanation of the Jacksonian period convincing. James Oakes declared himself "dazzled by the persuasive power" of Wilentz's argument that the Jefferson-Jackson political tradition was not questioning whether to embrace capitalism but rather "how decent or indecent American capitalism would be." In Oakes's estimation, "by reinterpreting the economic policy wars of the 1790s and 1830s as part of a larger fight for democracy itself," Wilentz had successfully demonstrated that there was "a strong case for the continuity of the early struggles against the Money Power with the later struggles against the Slave Power." In other words, the disputes over the First and Second Banks of the United States between Hamiltonians and Jeffersonians, in the former case, and Whigs and Jacksonians, in the latter case, delineated the coalitions that would fight over slavery in the years leading up to the Civil War.[30]

Other historians were not as enamored of Wilentz's *Rise of Democracy.* The criticisms centered on several critical issues that defined the Jacksonian period. For example, Wilentz suggested that while Thomas Jefferson remained "ambivalent" about slavery, he never made the leap that "slavery made white equality possible." Jefferson also "never tried to disown" antislavery Republicans. Wilentz seemed satisfied that these two points were enough to claim that "Jefferson and his party left an ambiguous but largely positive legacy," but his argument left Glenn Altschuler and John Patrick Diggins unconvinced. Wilentz had a similar take on Andrew Jackson. Old Hickory was "a benevolent, if realistic paternalist" when it came to Indian removal, a claim with which Altschuler and Jan Ellen Lewis took issue. The latter two historians also took Wilentz to task for accepting at face value the Jacksonian rhetoric. Wilentz proposed, for example, that "at bottom, the Jackson Democracy was chiefly what its proponents said it was." This acceptance of Jacksonian rhetoric as a description of motives and reality was problematic; as Altschuler opined, "*The Rise of Democracy* is better at spotting democratic rhetoric than in supplying the criteria for assessing the democratic content of specific policies."[31]

Wilentz's attempt at synthesizing the Age of Jackson appears to have been overshadowed by Daniel Walker Howe's *What Hath God Wrought: The Transformation of America, 1815-1848*. Despite his claim that his book "does not argue a thesis," Howe maintained that a "communications revolution" maximized the changes brought on by the market economy, the Second Great Awakening, and the development of the second American party system. This communications revolution included the development of electric telegraphy, the expansion of publishing (particularly newspapers), the growth of the postal system, and the concomitant transportation revolution, which witnessed the changes in travel associated with better roads and the development of steamboats, canals, and railroads. Entrepreneurs, preachers, and politicians alike understood the importance of the revolutionary changes in communications taking place and moved to take advantage of them to reach the general public with their messages of prosperity, sanctification, and democracy. While it is still too early to tell, the awarding of the 2008 Pulitzer Prize for history to Howe's study suggests that his interpretation of the Jacksonian period may have more historiographic influence than other recent works.[32]

The most recognizable recent biography of Jackson and treatment of the Jacksonian period, at least for the public, is Jon Meacham's *American Lion: Andrew Jackson in the White House*. Winner of the 2009 Pulitzer Prize for biography, *American Lion* was originally conceived as a study of Jackson's relationship with his cabinet but evolved into a study of Jackson the man as president. Meacham used readily available sources, as well as previously inaccessible sources in privately held collections, to tell the story of Jackson's often tumultuous relationship with his family, particularly Andrew and Emily Donelson, and the challenges that he faced as president. He argued, in words reminiscent of James Parton, that Old

Hickory "was the most contradictory of men." For example, he was "a champion of extending freedom and democracy to even the poorest of whites," but at the same time he "was an unrepentant slaveholder." He served as the guardian of three Native American children (Lyncoya, Charley, and Theodore), yet he was the driving force behind Indian removal in the 1830s. Meacham's prose is dramatic and personal in the sense that it draws the reader into the narrative to see the humanity of the historical personages. Aside from an interesting psychological analysis of Jackson's niece, Emily Donelson, historians will not find much new in *American Lion* and may even be put off by the personal details that seem to have made the book ubiquitous among the reading public. If he has done nothing else, however, Meacham has helped bring Jackson, and the period named after him, back into the public's view.[33]

Conclusion

It is clear that like many other schools of historiographic interpretation, Jacksonian historians have been influenced by the circumstances of their time. Patrician historians railed against the increasing democratization celebrated by Progressive historians, while ethnocultural historians examined sociocultural arguments during a time of severe social upheaval. Arthur M. Schlesinger Jr. responded to the myriad changes introduced by Franklin D. Roosevelt's New Deal programs, just as Daniel Walker Howe seemingly was affected by the rapid change in communications occurring in the decade before the publication of his work in 2006. The most fertile periods of Jacksonian historiography seem to come when scholars are wrestling with "the shape of democracy." Alexis de Tocqueville would not be surprised—nor should we.

NOTES

1. Alexis de Tocqueville, *Democracy in America,* ed. J. P. Mayer and trans. George Lawrence (New York: Perennial, 2000), 19; and Daniel Feller, "Rediscovering Jacksonian America," in *The State of U.S. History,* ed. Melvyn Stokes (Oxford: Berg, 2002), 84.

2. James Parton, *Life of Andrew Jackson,* 3 vols. (New York: Mason Brothers, 1861), 1:vii; and Charles G. Sellers Jr., "Andrew Jackson versus the Historians," *Mississippi Valley Historical Review* 44 (Mar. 1958): 615.

3. Sellers, "Andrew Jackson versus the Historians," 616-18.

4. Ibid., 618.

5. Frederick Jackson Turner, *The Frontier in American History* (1920; repr., New York: Henry Holt, 1953), 192, 302.

6. Sellers, "Andrew Jackson versus the Historians," 618-26; and Daniel Feller, "Politics and Society: Toward a Jacksonian Synthesis," *Journal of the Early Republic* 10 (Summer 1990): 136.

7. Sellers, "Andrew Jackson versus the Historians," 620-21; and John Spencer Bassett, *The Life of Andrew Jackson* (New York: Macmillan, 1916), 750.

8. Sellers, "Andrew Jackson versus the Historians," 623-24; and Thomas P. Abernethy, *From Frontier to Plantation in Tennessee: A Study in Frontier Democracy* (Chapel Hill: Univ. of North Carolina Press, 1932; repr., Tuscaloosa: Univ. of Alabama Press, 1967), 248-49.

9. Sellers, "Andrew Jackson versus the Historians," 626; and Alfred A. Cave, *Jacksonian Democracy and the Historians* (Gainesville: Univ. of Florida Press, 1964), 50-51.

10. Cave, *Jacksonian Democracy,* 54-59; Gerald N. Grob and George Athan Billias, eds., *Interpretations of American History: Patterns and Perspectives,* vol. 1, *To 1877,* 6th ed. (New York: Free Press, 1992), 260-61; Bray Hammond, review of *The Age of Jackson,* by Arthur M. Schlesinger Jr., *Journal of Economic History* 6 (May 1946): 79-84; Richard Hofstadter, *The American Political Tradition and the Men Who Made It* (New York: Knopf, 1948), 55; and Walter Hugins, *Jacksonian Democracy and the Working Class: A Study of the New York Workingmen's Movement, 1829-1837* (Palo Alto, Calif.: Stanford Univ. Press, 1960), 219-20.

11. Sean Wilentz, "On Class and Politics in Jacksonian America," *Reviews in American History* 10 (Dec. 1982): 46-47. The consensus school focused on what had united, rather than what had divided, Americans historically. Significant historians of this school included Daniel Boorstein, Louis Hartz, and Richard Hofstadter.

12. Feller, "Toward a Jacksonian Synthesis," 138-42.

13. Richard P. McCormick, "New Perspectives on Jacksonian Politics," *American Historical Review* 65 (Jan. 1960): 289; McCormick, *The Second American Party System: Party Formation in the Jacksonian Era* (Chapel Hill: Univ. of North Carolina Press, 1966); Frederick A. Ogg, *The Reign of Andrew Jackson*

(New Haven, Conn.: Yale Univ. Press, 1919), 114; Feller, "Toward a Jacksonian Synthesis," 140-41; and Edward Pessen, *Jacksonian America: Society, Personality, and Politics,* rev. ed. (Urbana: Univ. of Illinois Press, 1985), 97.

14. Marvin Meyers, *The Jacksonian Persuasion: Politics and Belief* (Palo Alto, Calif.: Stanford Univ. Press, 1957), 11, 13.

15. Michael Paul Rogin, *Fathers and Children: Andrew Jackson and the Subjugation of the American Indian* (New York: Knopf, 1975; repr., New Brunswick, N.J.: Transaction, 1991), xxv, 54, 10; and James C. Curtis, *Andrew Jackson and the Search for Vindication* (New York: HarperCollins, 1976), 10-12, 22-23.

16. John William Ward, *Andrew Jackson: Symbol for an Age* (New York: Oxford Univ. Press, 1955), 10, 209-10.

17. Bernard Bailyn, *The Ideological Origins of the American Revolution* (Cambridge, Mass.: Belknap Press of Harvard Univ. Press, 1967); Gordon S. Wood, *The Creation of the American Republic, 1776-1787* (Chapel Hill: Univ. of North Carolina Press, 1969; paperback ed., New York: W. W. Norton, 1972), 65-70, 596-615; and J. G. A. Pocock, *The Machiavellian Moment: Florentine Political Thought and the Atlantic Republican Tradition* (Princeton, N.J.: Princeton Univ. Press, 1975).

18. Robert V. Remini, *The Legacy of Andrew Jackson: Essays on Democracy, Indian Removal, and Slavery* (Baton Rouge: Louisiana State Univ. Press, 1988), 9-11; Remini, *Andrew Jackson and the Course of American Empire,* vol. 1 (New York: Harper and Row, 1977), 50, 80, 94; Remini, *Andrew Jackson and the Course of American Freedom,* vol. 2 (New York: Harper and Row, 1981), 76-78, 31; and Remini, *Andrew Jackson and the Course of American Democracy,* vol. 3 (New York: Harper and Row, 1984), 21-22.

19. William J. Cooper Jr., *The South and the Politics of Slavery, 1828-1856* (Baton Rouge: Louisiana State Univ. Press, 1978), xii-xv, 26-29; J. Mills Thornton III, *Politics and Power in a Slave Society: Alabama, 1800-1860* (Baton Rouge: Louisiana State Univ. Press, 1978); Harry L. Watson, *Jacksonian Politics and Community Conflict: The Emergence of the Second American Party System in Cumberland County, North Carolina* (Baton Rouge: Louisiana State Univ. Press, 1981); and Richard B. Latner, *The Presidency of Andrew Jackson, 1829-1837* (Athens: Univ. of Georgia Press, 1982), 23, 27.

20. Sean Wilentz, *Chants Democratic: New York City and the Rise of the American Working Class, 1788-1850* (New York: Oxford Univ. Press, 1984), 14, 63, 91-95, 237-45.

21. Harry L. Watson, *Liberty and Power: The Politics of Jacksonian America* (New York: Hill and Wang, 1990), 8-9, 43-45.

22. Sean Wilentz, "On Class and Politics," 58; and Watson, *Liberty and Power,* 28.

23. Melvyn Stokes and Stephen Conway, eds., *The Market Revolution in America: Social, Political, and Religious Expressions, 1800-1880* (Charlottes-

ville: Univ. Press of Virginia, 1996), 1; Charles Sellers, *The Market Revolution: Jacksonian America, 1815-1846* (Oxford: Oxford Univ. Press, 1991), 4, 32; and William G. Shade, review of *The Market Revolution: Jacksonian America, 1815-1846*, by Charles Sellers, *Journal of Economic History* 53 (June 1993): 429.

24. Stokes and Conway, eds., *Market Revolution in America*; and "A Symposium on Charles Sellers, *The Market Revolution: Jacksonian America, 1815-1846*," *Journal of the Early Republic* 12 (Winter 1992): 445-76.

25. Donald B. Cole, *The Presidency of Andrew Jackson* (Lawrence: Univ. Press of Kansas, 1993), 272; Anne C. Rose, *Voices of the Marketplace: American Thought and Culture, 1830-1860* (New York: Twayne, 1995), xvii; and Daniel Feller, *The Jacksonian Promise: America, 1815-1840* (Baltimore: Johns Hopkins Univ. Press, 1995), xii-xiv.

26. Daniel Feller, "The Market Revolution Ate My Homework," *Reviews in American History* 25 (Sept. 1997): 415; Christopher Clark, "The Consequences of the Market Revolution in the American North," in *The Market Revolution in America: Social, Political, and Religious Expressions, 1800-1880*, ed. Stokes and Conway, 29; Shade, review of *The Market Revolution*, 430; and Edward Pessen, review of *The Market Revolution: Jacksonian America, 1815-1846*, by Charles Sellers, *Journal of Southern History* 59 (Nov. 1993): 750.

27. Feller, "Rediscovering Jacksonian America," 69.

28. Hendrik Booraem, *Young Hickory: The Making of Andrew Jackson* (Dallas, Tex.: Taylor, 2001), xii; Andrew Burstein, *The Passions of Andrew Jackson* (New York: Knopf, 2003), xix-xx; H. W. Brands, *Andrew Jackson: His Life and Times* (New York: Doubleday, 2005); and Sean Wilentz, *Andrew Jackson* (New York: Henry Holt, 2005), 9, 12. For an extensive discussion of Burstein's biography, see Matthew S. Warshauer, review of *The Passions of Andrew Jackson*, by Andrew Burstein, *Tennessee Historical Quarterly* 63 (Winter 2003): 366-73.

29. Sean Wilentz, *The Rise of American Democracy: Jefferson to Lincoln* (New York: W. W. Norton, 2005), xvii, xx-xxi.

30. James Oakes, "The Age of Jackson and the Rise of American Democracies," *Journal of the Historical Society* 6 (Dec. 2006): 495-96.

31. Wilentz, *Rise of American Democracy*, 136-37, 324-25, 513; Glenn Altschuler, "Democracy as a Work in Progress," *Reviews in American History* 34 (June 2006): 171-73; John Patrick Diggins, "Democracy and Its Deceptions," *Journal of the Historical Society* 6 (Dec. 2006): 516-17; and Jan Ellen Lewis, "What We Talk about When We Talk about Democracy," *Journal of the Historical Society* 6 (Dec. 2006): 531-32.

32. Daniel Walker Howe, *What Hath God Wrought: The Transformation of America, 1815-1848* (Oxford: Oxford Univ. Press, 2006), 1-2, 3, 332, 695, 849.

33. Jon Meacham, *American Lion: Andrew Jackson in the White House* (New York: Random House, 2008), xxi, 164.

CHAPTER TWO

The Corrupt Bargain and the Rise of the Jacksonian Movement, 1825-1828

KRISTOFER RAY

Andrew Jackson was anxious in January 1825. He had surprised many in the previous fall's presidential election by garnering a plurality of the popular vote. No candidate won an electoral majority, however, which meant that the election would be decided by the House of Representatives. Jackson and his supporters expected to win the House runoff, but by late January rumors were swirling that his victory was not assured. Former presidential candidate and House Speaker, Henry Clay, some observers believed, had struck a deal with John Quincy Adams. In return for political considerations, Clay supposedly promised to throw his political weight (and the electoral votes of states he had won) behind Adams. By the end of January, Jackson was preparing for such a possibility. As he pointed out to William Berkeley Lewis, "I wrote you in great haste the other day in which I gave you the rumors that were in circulation of intrigue, union, and corruption about the Pl. election—I am told it has this morning developed itself, & that Mr Clay has come out in the open in support of Mr Adams—This, for one, I am pleased with—It shews that want of principle in all concerned—and how easy certain men can abandon principle, unite with political enemies for self agrandisement." It could be pleasing, Jackson believed, because such corruption would "give the people a full view of our political weathercocks here, and how little confidence ought to be reposed in the professions of some great political characters. One thing I know, intrigue cannot deprive me of . . . the high ground the people have placed me on." With that high ground he could return to Tennessee with his honor intact, carrying with him his "independence & my poli[ti]cal principles, pure & uncontaminated by bargain & sale, or combinations of any kind."[1]

Ultimately, the rumors seemed to prove accurate: Jackson lost the election to Adams in the House runoff, and not long thereafter Clay was named secretary of state. Whether or not a formal "bargain" took place, a political firestorm erupted. And although he was perhaps less sanguine than he had been when writing to Lewis, throughout the affair Jackson forcefully professed his integrity. "By me no plans were concerted to impair the pure principles of our Republican institutions," he wrote to supporter Samuel Swartwout, "or to frustrate that fundamental one which maintains the supremacy of the people's will; on the contrary, having never in any manner . . . interfered with the question, my conscience stands void of offence, and will go quietly with me, heedless of the insinuations of any, who thro management may seek an influence, not sanctioned by merit."[2]

Jackson and his supporters concluded that more would be necessary than merely the assertion of political honor, however. As Jackson made clear to Swartwout, the institutions binding the republic had been damaged by this "corrupt bargain" and would have to be restored lest the will of the people be undermined by aristocratic machinations. It is upon this notion that he and his supporters would build a remarkable organization—one that laid the groundwork for Jackson's victory in 1828.

In short, the corrupt bargain of 1825 became a launching point for the Jacksonian political movement. On this point virtually all modern historians agree. There are, moreover, related points that command a broad scholarly consensus: that the corrupt bargain gave an unfocused political theater a clarity that laid the foundation for what would become the second American party system and that Henry Clay's actions were not necessarily impure or corrupt, but that, given popular democratic realities by 1825, his political miscalculation was stunning.

Although its immediate causes stem from the 1824 election, the corrupt bargain grew more broadly out of the increasingly chaotic political and economic milieu of the late eighteenth and early nineteenth centuries. Indeed, in the decades after the Revolution, Americans had to come to terms with rapid political and economic development.[3] By the 1820s the country remained agrarian, but large-scale trans-Appalachian migration ensured that agricultural energies were becoming more diffuse while eastern business interests were beginning to coalesce. These developments led to an increase in internal market structures, which were particularly (though not exclusively) noticeable in the North.[4]

These internal economic structures gradually compelled farmers to move toward market production. In effect, it meant that yeomen who once had tried to remain subsistent or interdependent on kin, neighbors, and household production were now focusing on commercial markets, in the process becoming more dependent on manufactured goods and on obtaining money to help pay taxes, acquiring land for future generations, and reducing debt.[5] Radical changes in transportation helped facilitate these internal developments.

Political questions stemming from these economic forces took on particular importance in the wake of the Panic of 1819. Created by overextension of speculators in conjunction with unsound banking practices (most prevalent in the West, where speculators used "wildcat" banks to obtain paper money loans and secure vast tracts of land), the panic effectively served as a catalyst for more extensive popular democratic development. As historian Charles Sellers noted, the panic exacerbated the fears of a growing debtor class, which realized that interdependent networks of exchange would no longer offer protection against the whims of the boom-bust cycle. Through the panic/depression years, these people proved increasingly willing to express their concerns politically. In effect, market-related questions became core ingredients of political debate during the antebellum period.

The panic-related willingness to engage the political sphere came at a moment when that sphere was in a state of relative chaos. Federalism had collapsed as a national movement by 1820, and the remaining Jeffersonian Republican "party" found itself incapable of dealing with the varying interests contained beneath its umbrella. In the changing political milieu of the early nineteenth century, Republicans found themselves divided over the nature and meaning of economic development. More progressive elements looked to manufacturing and entrepreneurial innovation, were not opposed to creating state banks and maintaining a bank of the United States, and generally supported expansive development. Another element within the party adhered to a more hesitant economic philosophy. They favored vigorous development, to be sure, but they worried that the creation of state banks sacrificed general welfare for individual gain, strongly opposed the Bank of the United States, and feared what an expansive economy might do to the American debtor class, particularly in terms of land law and in light of catastrophes such as Jefferson's embargo of 1807-1809 or the Panic of 1819.[6]

These interest groups had not, as of 1824, worked themselves into national coalitions, however, meaning that ordinary Americans were struggling to comprehend the changing economy at a moment when the one remaining party could not formulate meaningful policy or organize behind any one leader. That year's presidential election reflected the political moment: with no clear front-runner, four Republican candidates emerged, regional in orientation and divided on questions of progress. As Harry Watson reminds us, evolving commitments to popular democracy would become far better organized in the wake of the contest.[7]

John Quincy Adams, Henry Clay, Andrew Jackson, and William H. Crawford (the chosen candidate of the once critical, but increasingly irrelevant, congressional caucus) all sought the presidency in 1824. Adams and Clay both embraced expansive definitions of progress, aligning themselves with policies Clay trumpeted as the American System. Among other things, it included support for and defense of a bank of the United States, a protective tariff, and federal support for internal improvements, to be funded by proceeds of land sales. Jackson, meanwhile, expressed ambivalence toward programs of internal improvements. He supported such measures on the state level, as his state and local career showed, but as president he later opposed them at the national level.[8] Crawford, by contrast, was open in his opposition to American System-type programs.

The positions maintained by this mixture of candidates showed how Republicans could no longer unify behind a single person or issue. This splintering had a direct effect on the election, as William L. Barney noted: with no party mechanisms to focus voter identification, the rival candidates canceled each other out.[9] Jackson, thanks to his reputation as the "Hero of New Orleans," ultimately won 43 percent of the popular vote. No candidate received a majority of electoral votes, however. Thus, as the Constitution requires, the election would be decided by the House of Representatives.

The House runoff was not as wide open as it would appear. The provisions of the Twelfth Amendment to the Constitution allow only the three top vote getters to participate in a runoff, which meant that Clay, who had come in fourth, was eliminated. Nor, with the exception of his closest supporters, was Crawford perceived to be a meaningful candidate, having suffered a debilitating stroke during the presidential campaign. So, in effect, the runoff became a de facto race between Adams and Jackson. And as Robert V. Remini noted, Henry Clay as Speaker of the House held the "awesome power" of being able to affect the outcome. It came as no surprise, given their broad agreement on matters of nationalism and internal development, that by January 1825 Clay had decided that Adams should emerge victorious.[10]

Feelers to this effect were sent out by Clay in late 1824 and early 1825, when Clay's lieutenant, Robert Letcher, made Adams aware that the Speaker might use his influence to ensure Adams's victory. In return, Clay wanted what Remini called "a prominent share in the administration," something Adams understood to mean the position of secretary of state. Although no evidence of a formal arrangement has surfaced, and Adams certainly disliked Clay personally, the sitting secretary of state understood Letcher's suggestion and silently acquiesced to it in the interest of his own advancement. Adams and Clay met in early January 1825, as Adams noted in his diary, which made no mention of any sort of official bargain. According to Remini, there simply "was no need. Both men understood each other's purposes and needs."[11]

But if there is no evidence of a formal agreement, rumors of a bargain almost immediately began to swirl through Washington. By mid-January, Clay faced sharp criticism on multiple fronts: in print, by Jackson supporters, and even by leaders in his home state (Kentucky's delegation had been ordered by its state legislature to vote for Jackson, which Clay ignored).[12] Clay strongly denounced the criticism, at one point even challenging to a duel a nameless individual who had besmirched his honesty in an essay published in the *Columbian Observer.* But the rumors would not abate. By the end of the month, Jackson was commenting on how, should credible evidence of a bargain appear, such a situation might play to his advantage.

The subsequent House vote seemed to validate the charge of "corrupt bargain." According to the rules, thirteen states would be needed to secure the election, and each state delegation would have one vote. When the House runoff began, Adams understood that he could depend on ten states: six from New England plus those states delivered by Clay (Kentucky, Ohio, Missouri, and Louisiana). As it turned out, Illinois and Maryland both went for Adams on the first ballot, which gave him twelve. Meanwhile, Jackson seemed to control seven states: Tennessee, South Carolina, New Jersey, Pennsylvania, Indiana, Alabama, and Mississippi. William Crawford's supporters secured four states for their candidate: Delaware, Georgia, Virginia, and North Carolina.

The outcome of the election in New York, whose delegation was divided, proved more difficult to predict. Martin Van Buren hoped the contention might work in William Crawford's favor: the greater the number of inconclusive ballots, the more reasonably could Crawford be offered as a compromise candidate. But on the first ballot something unexpected happened. Representative Stephen Van Rensselaer voted in favor of Adams, which gave Adams a majority in the New York delegation and thus the thirteenth and final state necessary for election. Days later the president-elect offered Clay the position of secretary of state, and when Clay accepted, the "bargain" seemed to have been sealed.

There is a general uniformity of agreement on Clay's motivation in supporting Adams: however poorly it turned out for him, Clay had no nefarious intention to corrupt American institutions. Daniel Feller, for example, notes that "the Adams-Clay 'bargain' did not lack honesty (Clay's belief in Jackson's unfitness was sincere, and his own qualifications for the state department were unquestioned)."[13] John Larson agrees. "Legitimate considerations," he explains, "could just as well have moved Clay supporters towards Adams without any reference to the makeup of the cabinet, and Clay was a logical choice for the State Department job."[14] To this point, Clay himself would add his belief that Jackson was unfit for the presidency and had the potential to become an American Napoleon. "As a friend of liberty, & to the permanence of our institutions," he wrote to Francis Brooke, "I cannot consent, in this early stage of their existence, by contributing to the election of a military chieftain, to give the strongest guarranty that this republic will march in the fatal road which has conducted every other republic to ruin."[15]

Policy considerations also figured prominently in Clay's decision, argued Robert V. Remini and Sean Wilentz. As Remini pointed out, siding with Adams would "mean the union of eastern with western interests with Clay's American System, thus providing the system with a *national* constituency."[16] Wilentz, who agrees, wrote that "by joining his supporters to those of the national candidate most like himself, Clay was promoting what he considered a credible divination of the democratic will as endorsing nationalist programs."[17] Charles Sellers makes clear that Clay knew "that his decision would realign the building blocks of national politics. By casting his lot with Adams, he was opting for a political economy allying the newer northwestern centers of market energy with the market's dynamic northeastern core to realize the American System's developmental program. He was positioning himself to lead the republic into its capitalist destiny."[18]

Sellers's point reminds us of another consideration: Clay's ambition. Although he concedes that Clay "genuinely feared to trust republicanism to the Napoleon of the woods," Sellers nevertheless argues that "reinforcing this high minded objection was the pragmatic consideration that a Kentuckian was more likely to reach the presidency in succession to an easterner than to another westerner."[19] Similarly, Richard E. Ellis has noted that Clay "feared Jackson as a formidable rival for western support, and he did not believe Jackson had either the experience or the temperament to be a good president. He also correctly believed that Jackson was no friend of the American System."[20] Concludes Remini, "Those who claimed to understand Clay best credited his decision to accept the office of secretary of state to his ambition—his overreaching ambition."[21]

In effect, then, there is a basic consensus among modern historians. On the one hand, they concede that it is unlikely that there ever was a formal understanding between Clay and Adams— that, as Remini wrote, contemporary "observers chose to believe what they found most congenial to their personal instincts and feelings."[22] On the other hand, as Daniel Feller makes clear, Clay deserved criticism for his lack of "political sagacity. A campaign in which responding to popular sentiment had become the highest imperative ended with an arrangement that stank of collusion against the people's will. Charges of conspiracy and illegitimacy tainted the Adams presidency from its birth."[23] Sean Wilentz went a step further, arguing that Clay's actions stemmed from a fundamental flaw. "If, in politics, a blunder is worse than a crime," he argued, "then Clay, along with Adams, was guilty indeed, of a complete failure of political intelligence and imagination. That Clay only gradually came to understand what went wrong only proved the failure's magnitude. By his own lights, he had acted with patriotic correctness, even statesmanship."[24]

As these scholars point out, the charge of corruption proved devastating for Clay and Adams and essential to the formation of

the Jacksonian political movement. To Jackson and his supporters, the meaning was clear and critical: organization of the electorate would be essential to overturn an aristocratically inclined
regime that had subverted the popular will and undermined
America's republican institutions. This belief reinforces that the
"bargain" took place along what had become a fault line between
conceptions of republican leadership. As Wilentz implied, Clay
saw himself as acting within the parameters of the traditions laid
out by the framers of the Republic: that virtuous statesmen should
act out of prudent deliberation rather than becoming, as Adams
warned in his first message to Congress, "palsied by the will of
our constituents."[25] By contrast, observed Harry Watson, Jackson
believed that "'the great body of the people' was honest and virtuous, while those who claimed the privileges of the elite were
likely to be selfish and corrupt. He sought to protect what he regarded as the liberty of the many against the designs of the few."[26]
This mandate to protect justified immediate action. As Michael
Holt argued, charges of bargain and corruption thus "stigmatized
the administration as privileged enemies of the popular will and
greatly increased the credibility of the Jacksonian cause."[27]

Through the bargain, as Remini put it, "the General's friends
had found an issue with which to bludgeon the incoming administration and replace it in four years with the 'virtuous' hero of
the Revolution and War of 1812."[28] Jacksonian displeasure was so
strong that it brought focus to the chaotic political arena in which
Americans had operated since the collapse of the Federalist movement. As Daniel Walker Howe observed, subsequent agitation
signaled "the end of nonparty politics, [and] the foundation for
the party system that was to come."[29] Michael Holt agreed, noting
that in the years "between 1824 and 1828 a new alignment among
politicians and voters began to crystallize."[30]

This crystallization was most apparent through the efforts
of Jacksonians. For four years Jackson and his allies nationwide
worked to ensure that the recipients of the corrupt bargain would
not stay in office beyond their one term. They left Congress in
a state of paralysis, such that, as Andrew Burstein wrote, "Little

would get done. . . . Congress, after 1825, was simply looking ahead to 1828."[31] Meanwhile, Jackson's and his colleagues' efforts to put together the "Nashville committee" helped organize the movement more broadly.[32] Harry Watson and William Barney added that this organization depended on the energies of increasingly sophisticated state-level politicians.[33] Particularly, Martin Van Buren and other former Crawford supporters played vital roles in the evolving Jacksonian movement. According to Van Buren, strong organization was the only way to win elections and defend American republicanism. To succeed in 1828, party strife of the type not seen for many years would be necessary. Otherwise, politics would devolve into a corrupt and unseemly scramble of personal rivalries, as had happened in 1824. Or worse, perhaps, sectional rivalries might come to the fore, such as those seen in the Missouri crisis.[34] By 1828, Jacksonians were employing myriad political cultural tools to avoid these pitfalls: newspaper networks, campaign workers to "bring out the vote," county and district conventions to nominate candidates, physical symbols such as hickory sticks and buttons with which ordinary Americans could identify their candidate, and rallies and barbecues.[35]

The end result of Jacksonian organization was remarkable; whereas in 1824, 26 percent of eligible voters came out to vote, in 1828, 56 percent came out to vote. Jackson, meanwhile, carried every state from Pennsylvania south and west (except Maryland and Delaware) and defeated Adams in a landslide.[36] The Jacksonian movement had been born.

So what can be learned from the corrupt bargain? Two things, it seems. As noted earlier, the bargain spawned the Jacksonian movement, and in less organized fashion that of the National Republicans. Ultimately this organization would lead to the second American party system. But, on another level, the bargain reinforced the argument that in the first quarter of the nineteenth century a new political and socioeconomic environment evolved that altered the way politics was done. And this, argues Sean Wilentz, is why Clay's miscalculation is so stunning. Simply put, "Clay did not comprehend how much and how quickly the rules were changing in the 1820s along majoritarian lines."[37] Clay and others, both contemporary and modern, could counter that the framers of the Constitution had not intended for the new United States to be a democracy and thus that his actions were appropriate for one committed to notions of republican government. But that argument, as Robert V. Remini noted, was irrelevant by 1825. Even if the framers had not intended the popular vote to determine presidential elections, the reality is that "the nation was fast evolving from a republic to a democracy. The Industrial Revolution, market revolution, and transportation revolution had helped trigger the phenomenon."[38]

Basic political demography reinforces Remini's contention of political energy. Between 1800 and 1824, the number of states increased from sixteen to twenty-four, and with them grew the importance of the electorate. In 1800, only two states determined electors by popular vote, whereas by 1824 a majority did so. By 1832, only South Carolina continued to select electors through the state legislature. Suffrage was basically universal for white males over twenty-one by 1824, compared with thirty years before when various state-level property restrictions limited voting to 70 percent of the population.[39]

And unlike in 1800, in 1824 the lack of any meaningful opposition meant that the electorate was unstructured by party discipline. As William Barney put it, the mass electorate was "an immense prize" for any group that could mobilize it, and the corrupt bargain became the perfect tool around which to begin this mobilization.[40] The bargain was thus crucial because it helped fuse and focus two-plus decades of political and economic energy. It became, as Remini makes clear, "the single event that drove men—Jackson especially—to a more pronounced democratic position and ended forever the notion that representatives are somehow free agents to decide by themselves the public good."[41] Subsequent public outcry in effect became "one of moral outrage against a coalition brought to power in total disregard of the popular will."[42]

These points have become so well established that scholars have used them to form a basic consensus on the corrupt bargain. As such, there is little in the way of a broader body of literature;

most historians allot the bargain only a few paragraphs or pages before moving on to issues related to Jackson's presidential policies. And this in turn leads to a question: Why is there not more coverage of an event Jacksonians felt was so absolutely essential? Perhaps there is enough room for a new generation of scholars to consider the question and bring light to a critical but often glossed over aspect of Jacksonian history.

NOTES

Special thanks to Brian Steele and Harry Watson for their insightful commentary/criticism.

1. Andrew Jackson to William Berkeley Lewis, Jan. 24, 1825, in *The Papers of Andrew Jackson,* vol. 6, *1825-1828,* ed. Harold Moser (Knoxville: Univ. of Tennessee Press, 2002), 20.

2. Jackson to Samuel Swartwout, in *Andrew Jackson vs. Henry Clay: Democracy and Development in Antebellum America,* ed. Harry L. Watson (Boston: Bedford/St. Martin, 1998), 159-60.

3. See, for example, Sean Wilentz, *The Rise of American Democracy: Jefferson to Lincoln* (New York: W. W. Norton, 2005); Daniel Walker Howe, *What Hath God Wrought: The Transformation of America, 1815-1848* (Oxford: Oxford Univ. Press, 2006); John Larson, *Internal Improvement: National Public Works and the Promise of Popular Government in the Early United States* (Chapel Hill: Univ. of North Carolina Press, 2001); Melvyn Stokes and Stephen Conway, eds., *The Market Revolution in America: Social, Political, and Religious Expressions, 1800-1880* (Charlottesville: Univ. Press of Virginia, 1996); Charles Sellers, *The Market Revolution: Jacksonian America, 1815-1846* (Oxford: Oxford Univ. Press, 1991); William L. Barney, *The Passage of the Republic: An Interdisciplinary History of Nineteenth-Century America* (Lexington, Mass.: DC Heath and Company, 1987); and Steven Watts, *The Republic Reborn: War and the Making of Liberal America, 1790-1820* (Baltimore: Johns Hopkins Univ. Press, 1987).

4. As to trans-Appalachian migration, after 1815 approximately 60,000 people a year went west, according to William Barney. See Barney, *Passage of the Republic,* 10. Similar economic development was occurring in the early nineteenth-century South, to be sure. See Harry L. Watson, *Jacksonian Politics and Community Conflict: The Emergence of the Second American Party System in Cumberland County, North Carolina* (Baton Rouge: Louisiana State Univ. Press, 1981); Daniel Dupre, *Transforming the Cotton Frontier: Madison County, Alabama, 1800-1840* (Baton Rouge: Louisiana State Univ. Press, 1997); Craig Thompson Friend, *Along the Maysville Road: The Early American Republic in the Trans-Appalachian West* (Knoxville: Univ. of Tennessee Press, 2005); Kristofer Ray, *Middle*

Tennessee, 1775–1825: Progress and Popular Democracy on the Southwestern Frontier (Knoxville: Univ. of Tennessee Press, 2007); and Tom Downey, *Planting a Capitalist South: Masters, Merchants, and Manufacturers in the Southern Interior, 1790–1860* (Baton Rouge: Louisiana State Univ. Press, 2005).

5. See, for example, Christopher Clark, *The Roots of Rural Capitalism: Western Massachusetts, 1780–1860* (Ithaca, N.Y.: Cornell Univ. Press, 1990); Sellers, *Market Revolution;* Harry L. Watson, *Liberty and Power: The Politics of Jacksonian America* (New York: Hill and Wang, 1990); and Barney, *Passage of the Republic.*

6. On reactions to the embargo, see Ray, *Middle Tennessee, 1775–1825,* chap. 5. On increasing economic divisions in the early nineteenth century, see Richard Ellis, "The Market Revolution and the Transformation of American Politics, 1801–1837," in *The Market Revolution in America,* ed. Stokes and Conway, 149–76; Lawrence A. Peskin, "How the Republicans Learned to Love Manufacturing: The First Parties and the 'New Economy,'" *Journal of the Early Republic* 22 (Summer 2002): 235–62. Larson, *Internal Improvement;* and Andrew Shankman, *Crucible of American Democracy: The Struggle to Fuse Egalitarianism and Capitalism in Jeffersonian Pennsylvania* (Lawrence: Univ. Press of Kansas, 2004). On western issues, see, for example, Richard Ellis, *The Jeffersonian Crisis: Courts and Politics in the Young Republic* (New York: Oxford Univ. Press, 1971); Friend, *Along Maysville Road;* Dupre, *Transforming the Cotton Frontier;* and Ray, *Middle Tennessee, 1775–1825.*

7. Watson, *Liberty and Power,* chap. 3. Popular democracy as a force had emerged in the 1790s and helped create the first American party system. See, for example, Simon Newman, *Parades and the Politics of the Street: Festive Culture in the Early American Republic* (Philadelphia: Univ. of Pennsylvania Press, 1997).

8. Watson, *Andrew Jackson vs. Henry Clay,* 62–63ff.

9. Barney, *Passage of the Republic,* 133–34. See also Watson, *Liberty and Power,* chap. 3.

10. Robert V. Remini, *Henry Clay: Statesman for the Union* (New York: W. W. Norton, 1991), 253; and Wilentz, *Rise of American Democracy,* 254.

11. Remini, *Henry Clay,* 255–57, 258.

12. Adams made "bargains" with other people, to be sure. For example, John Scott, the lone delegate from Missouri, voted for Adams after having received reassurances about printing patronage. Moreover, remaining Federalists in Maryland and Massachusetts turned to Adams after he made it clear that Federalists would not be excluded from power. But given the reputations of the players in question, as well as the positions of power at stake, rumors of a bargain between Adams and Clay were bound to make news. And make news it did: as Sean Wilentz and others have noted, less than two weeks before the House runoff charges of corruption were being widely published. Wilentz, *Rise of American Democracy,* 255.

13. Daniel Feller, *The Jacksonian Promise: America, 1815–1840* (Baltimore: Johns Hopkins Univ. Press, 1995), 69–70.

14. Larson, *Internal Improvement,* 157.

15. Henry Clay to Francis Brooke, Jan. 28, 1825, in Watson, *Andrew Jackson vs. Henry Clay,* 158.

16. Remini, *Henry Clay,* 254.

17. Wilentz, *Rise of American Democracy,* 255-56.

18. Sellers, *Market Revolution,* 198.

19. Ibid.

20. Ellis, "Market Revolution and the Transformation of American Politics," 167-68.

21. Remini, *Henry Clay,* 270.

22. Ibid.

23. Feller, *Jacksonian Promise,* 69-70.

24. Wilentz, *Rise of American Democracy,* 255-56.

25. John Quincy Adams, First Message to Congress, Dec. 6, 1825, Miller Center for Public Affairs, University of Virginia, http://millercenter.org/scripps/archive/speeches/detail/3514.

26. Watson, *Andrew Jackson vs. Henry Clay,* 20.

27. Michael Holt, *The Rise and Fall of the American Whig Party: Jacksonian Politics and the Onset of the Civil War* (Oxford: Oxford Univ. Press, 1999), 7.

28. Remini, *Henry Clay,* 270.

29. Howe, *What Hath God Wrought,* 210.

30. Holt, *Rise and Fall of the American Whig Party,* 7.

31. Andrew Burstein, *America's Jubilee, July 4, 1826: A Generation Remembers the Revolution after Fifty Years of Independence* (New York: Vintage, 2001), 156.

32. See Moser, *Papers of Andrew Jackson,* vol. 6.

33. Barney, *Passage of the Republic,* 137; Watson, *Liberty and Power,* chap. 3.

34. Watson, *Andrew Jackson vs. Henry Clay,* 67.

35. Barney, *Passage of the Republic,* 139.

36. Ibid.

37. Wilentz, *Rise of American Democracy,* 256. See also Burstein, *America's Jubilee,* 147; and Paul Johnson, *The Early American Republic, 1789-1829* (New York: Oxford Univ. Press, 2007), 150-51.

38. Remini, *Henry Clay,* 260.

39. Barney, *Passage of the Republic,* 136. For more on evolving voting rights, see Alexander Keyssar, *The Right to Vote: The Contested History of Democracy in the United States* (New York: Basic Books, 2000).

40. Barney, *Passage of the Republic,* 136.

41. Robert V. Remini, *The Legacy of Andrew Jackson: Essays on Democracy, Indian Removal, and Slavery* (Baton Rouge: Louisiana State Univ. Press, 1988), 14. Quoted in John Ashworth, *Slavery, Capitalism, and Politics in the Antebellum Republic,* vol. 1, *Commerce and Compromise, 1820-1850* (Cambridge: Cambridge Univ. Press, 1995), 370.

42. Remini, *Henry Clay,* 270, 269.

CHAPTER THREE

Historians and the Nature of Party Politics in Jacksonian America

WADE SHAFFER

The origins of the modern American political system can be traced to the events of the 1830s and 1840s. Strict party discipline, the spoils system, political nominating conventions, elaborate electioneering, and the presidential ticket all originated with the second party system. It should not be surprising, then, that historians have long sought to understand the essential nature of politics in the Jacksonian period. Did it usher in the age of the common man? Were the party battles between the Democrats and the Whigs epic struggles between the forces of democracy and aristocracy? Should the period be viewed as the Age of Jackson, or has his influence been exaggerated? Finally, historians have argued over the connection, if any, between the political activities of the era and the coming of the Civil War. The history of Jacksonian politics, still fiercely contested, has produced some of the best and most important historical writing of the last sixty years.

Modern scholarship on Jacksonian politics begins with Arthur M. Schlesinger Jr.'s *The Age of Jackson*.[1] Schlesinger reframed the debate over Andrew Jackson and the second party system by portraying Jackson as the hero of the "common man" who fought valiantly against the moneyed elite. The Democratic Party that Jackson and Martin Van Buren created squared off against Henry Clay's and Daniel Webster's Whig Party, which represented the interests of conservatives and the wealthy. Heavily influenced by the Progressive historians Charles Beard and Frederick Jackson Turner and by the New Deal, Schlesinger saw class and ideology as the central dynamic of the era. Jackson—like Washington, Lincoln, and FDR—came to power during a period of great turmoil and uncertainty and became a great statesman by rising to the challenges of the day. His greatest victories came in ending the threat of nullification and breaking the economic death grip that the Bank of the United States held on the country. Under Jackson's leadership, the United States became a fairer, more democratic society where the average man had a chance not only to survive but to flourish. Schlesinger's account of the period, beautifully written and full of wonderful anecdotes and keen insights, remains essential reading. But it is also deeply flawed because Schlesinger essentially ignored race, class, and gender in his discussions. His "common man" was an adult white male, and Schlesinger had little to say about the willingness of Jackson and of both parties to allow slavery to thrive in a democratic society.

Schlesinger's work quickly drew responses from other historians. Richard Hofstadter devoted two chapters of *The American Political Tradition and the Men Who Made It* to the Jacksonian period.[2] Rejecting the idea that Jackson stood at the head of a "radical leveling movement," Hofstadter insisted that when Old Hickory and his supporters went after the Bank of the United States, they did so because they sought more credit and less control from the powerful national institution. As "expectant capitalists," Jacksonians included "rural capitalists and village entrepreneurs" who articulated the "philosophy of a rising middle class." The values of Democrats and Whigs were not that different; both were committed to capitalism and equalitarian democracy. Hofstadter's book helped spark consensus history, although he was never completely comfortable with that label.

Louis Hartz's influential *The Liberal Tradition in America: An Interpretation of American Political Thought since the Revolution* also emphasized the similarities between the Democrats and the Whigs.[3] According to Hartz, the Lockean liberalism that permeated political thought in America profoundly influenced members of both parties; the Whigs were merely the "wealthier, conservative strand in the liberal movement." The period was marked by two impulses, one toward democracy and the other toward capitalism. Since capitalism is "bound to be democratic," writes Hartz, these impulses should have operated hand in hand rather than touching off the bitter party battles and "massive confusion of political thought" that marked the era. Hartz's liberal synthesis fits nicely with Hofstadter's consensus interpretation, and both were widely accepted for decades.

Marvin Meyers continued the assault on Schlesinger's assertion that the spread of democracy and class consciousness were the keys to explaining the period. In *The Jacksonian Persuasion: Politics and Beliefs,* Meyers focused not on partisan rhetoric but on the complex and even contradictory set of moral beliefs that bound Americans together at this time.[4] While Jacksonians embraced the emerging liberal capitalist society, they also yearned to preserve or restore the "moral health" of the nation by honoring and propping up the "pristine yeoman agricultural society" of the Old Republic. Like Hartz, Meyers seemed puzzled by the contradictory nature of the political beliefs of this generation of Americans.

In the 1960s and 1970s historians turned to an "ethnocultural" explanation of party membership and ideology. Lee Benson pioneered this theory in *The Concept of Jacksonian Democracy: New York as a Test Case.*[5] Benson viewed narrative histories like *The Age of Jackson* as outdated and unscientific. By employing the research methods of the social sciences, historians could get closer to the truth. Data and multivariate analysis, not lofty prose, was needed to understand the past. Benson's data led him to discount entirely the notion that the Jacksonians championed the "common man" and fought to expand political participation and democratic reform. Nor were the Whigs reactionary conservatives struggling in vain to hold back the tidal wave of egalitarianism set in motion by Jackson's rise to power. The data also indicated that party membership stemmed from a complex set of factors, most notably religion, ethnicity, and cultural values and beliefs. Class and ideology mattered little; Whigs and Democrats were both entrepreneurs out to make a fast buck. Benson's deft and insistent use of social science research methodology persuaded many historians of the need to reexamine American political history with an eye toward highlighting the importance of social and moral dimensions of partisan activity. Ronald P. Formisano adapted Benson's ethnocultural interpretation to Michigan in an influential state study titled *The Birth of Mass Political Parties: Michigan, 1827-1861,* while Robert Kelley applied it at the national level in *The Cultural Pattern of American Politics: The First Century.*[6] Two key studies on the issuing of banking also employed an ethnocultural approach. William G. Shade's *Banks or No Banks: The Money Issue in Western Politics, 1832-1865* and James Roger Sharp's *The Jacksonians versus the Banks: Politics in the States after the Panic of 1837* used social science methodology to prove that banking developed into an issue that rigidly divided Whigs and Democrats.[7] But those divisions did not break down along class lines. Members of both parties aggressively pursued economic gain; they merely differed on the role of a national bank in assisting in their quest for wealth.

The "new political historians" of the same period also relied on quantitative research and social science methodology but reached different conclusions about the period. Richard P. McCormick argued in *The Second American Party System: Party Formation in the Jacksonian Era* that the quadrennial presidential elections were what animated Jacksonian politics and bound party members together.[8] Regional identity helped explain support for the Democrats or the Whigs, but ideology and constitutional issues did not. In fact, the leaders of the two parties worked assiduously to bury ideology and discussion over touchy subjects such as the extension of slavery into the western territories. Spectacle and pageantry in the presidential contests between 1824 and 1840 created the second party system, and both the Whig and the Democratic parties were "organized from the top downward." The essays in the edited volume by William Nisbet Chambers and Walter Dean Burnham, *The American Party Systems: Stages of Political Development,* supported McCormick's contention and helped establish the "party period" concept of explaining nineteenth-century political history.[9] Joel H. Silbey distilled three decades of research on the topic in *The American Political Nation, 1838-1893*.[10] The Democrats and Whigs emerged in Silbey's book as tightly controlled national political parties bound together by principles and policies that engendered fierce loyalty from their adherents. By 1840 the "parties had become communities," and the members of these communities insisted on being kept well informed and playing an active role in party affairs.

Taken together, the consensus historians associated with Hofstadter and the ethnocultural historians associated with Benson succeeded in demolishing the Progressive argument that class mattered much in the Jacksonian period. Their works, along with the studies conducted by the new political historians, moved ethnic and religious conflict to the fore and essentially marginalized class and economic conflict in the 1830s and 1840s. This interpretation—though sometimes challenged by iconoclastic scholars such as Edward Pessen, whose *Jacksonian America: Society, Personality, and Politics* offered a Marxist interpretation of the era, or Major L. Wilson, author of the overlooked *Space, Time and Freedom: The Quest for National Identity and the Irrepressible Conflict, 1815-1861*—held firm through the 1970s and worked to diminish interest in the political history of the era among the growing ranks of social and cultural historians.[11] But as social historians developed a more sophisticated and nuanced definition of class and culture, and as they explored the myriad ways in which American society changed during this period, they began to criticize the existing paradigm and to present another view of Jacksonian politics. It seemed highly improbable that seismic changes in the way society was ordered would not be reflected in the way that political affairs were conducted.

An early and ultimately unsuccessful attempt to blend social and political history involved the concept of modernization, first presented by Richard D. Brown in *Modernization: The Transformation of American Life, 1600-1865*.[12] Brown argued that the story of early American history was the wrenching transformation from a traditional to a modern society, but his theory has been criticized for being ahistorical and for oversimplifying an enormously complex and often contradictory process. Since both the Whig and the Democratic parties contained elements that were traditional and modern, this approach proved less than helpful in delineating differences between the two. Daniel Walker Howe had more success in applying aspects of modernization theory to his study of the Whig Party titled *The Political Culture of the American Whigs*.[13] He demonstrated that while the Whigs embraced economic development and "regarded the machine as an agent of redemption," their Democratic counterparts, skeptical and fearful of the changing economic realities of the day, "preferred the uniformity of a society of small farmers and artisans." Howe made no secret of his admiration for the Whigs and his disapproval of the Democrats, a theme he would return to often in his works. He echoed Meyers's assessment of the transitional nature of the era, with Americans simultaneously embracing the new socioeconomic order and clinging to their agrarian past. This interpretation has held up well over the years but is not without its critics.

Howe's work also revealed that the heated debate over the influence of classical republican thought on the Revolutionary era and the early Republic had spilled over into the Jacksonian period. Bernard Bailyn, J. G. A. Pocock, Gordon Wood, and other social and cultural historians of the late 1960s and 1970s laid siege to the prevailing liberal consensus paradigm of American politics. They argued that classical republican values such as virtue, civic humanism, and equality shaped political ideology and popular thought in the age of the American Revolution far more than Lockean liberalism. Soon their followers began to build a case that eighteenth-century republican thought continued to hold sway in Jeffersonian and Jacksonian America. Seminal works on the early Republic include Linda Kerber's *Federalists in Dissent: Ideology and Imagery in Jeffersonian America*, Lance Banning's *The Jeffersonian Persuasion*, and Drew McCoy's *The Elusive Republic: Political Economy in Jeffersonian America*.[14] For studies that stress the importance of republicanism in the Age of Jackson, consult, among many others, Howe's work on the Whigs; Harry L. Watson, *Jacksonian Politics and Community Conflict: The Emergence of the Second American Party System in Cumberland County, North Carolina;* and Major Wilson, "Republicanism and the Idea of Party in the Jacksonian Period."[15] Wilson concluded that "party spokesman used the language of republicanism to make sense of the rapidly changing world around them." Marc W. Kruman expanded upon this argument in "The Second American Party System and the Transformation of Revolutionary Republicanism."[16]

The idea that republicanism still mattered in the 1830s and 1840s seemed to explain some of the contradictory impulses of the period that had left Hartz and others baffled. Republican thought did not flow unaltered through the Jacksonian landscape. The startling transformations in transportation, economics, and social relations that characterized the period reshaped the way in which Americans viewed their republican heritage. Increasingly, they sought to reconcile this ideology of the past with the emerging liberal capitalist state that they were creating. This fundamental tension shaped both partisan debate and the behavior of political actors. Eventually the Jacksonian parties resolved this tension by constructing what Sean Wilentz has described as a "specific conception of republican politics, one that combined republican rhetoric with a post-Madisonian liberalism," or, more succinctly, "liberal republicanism."[17]

While the lingering influence of republicanism in the mid-nineteenth century was being systematically explored, social historians began to broaden the scope of political history by adding previously unheard voices to the conversation. To this point, discussions of Jacksonian politics had almost exclusively focused on the thoughts and actions of adult white men, who were, after all, essentially the only people allowed to vote at this time. But given the intensity of political activities and the emergence of the popular press, was it wise to limit historical discussions of the political world to those who could vote and run for office? Jurgen Habermas's notion of the public sphere allowed historians to chart the role of women and other disenfranchised peoples in the political milieu of the mid-nineteenth century. Far from being disengaged or marginal players, many white women participated actively in a variety of political activities, including petitioning, public speaking, and campaigning. This discovery necessitated the revision of the separate sphere theory articulated by Barbara Welter and others. It now appeared that many women moved freely and comfortably in the male-dominated sphere of politics. Mary P. Ryan laid out this argument in *Women in Public: Between Banners and Ballots, 1825-1880,* and Elizabeth R. Varon amplified it in *We Mean to Be Counted: White Women and Politics in Antebellum Virginia.*[18] Also essential to understanding women and politics in the period is Nancy Isenberg's *Sex and Citizenship in Antebellum America.*[19] Since both of the major parties of the period tolerated and even embraced racism, African Americans tended to support other parties such as the Liberty, Free Soil, and Republican. Few blacks could vote at this time, but they found other ways to enter the political arena. Frederick Douglass, Henry Highland Garnet, and other black abolitionists not only led the movement to end slavery but spoke on the campaign trail and threw their support behind like-minded candidates. Leon Litwack's pathbreaking *North of Slavery: The Negro in the Free States, 1790-1860* offers proof of the political activities of free blacks, and David W. Blight's sensitive study of *Frederick Douglass' Civil War: Keeping Faith in Jubilee* documents the problems that the black leader sometimes had in supporting the Republicans.[20]

The appeal of third parties to those on the margins of American political life has been well documented. The Anti-Masons, the Liberty Party, the Free Soil Party, and the Know-Nothings all attracted followers during the Jacksonian period with a message of antipartyism. The Whigs and the Democrats, tightly ruled by corrupt and bloated career politicians, cared only about the status quo and about getting more time at the public trough. Deeply rooted suspicion of political parties was not limited to third-party supporters, however. Gerald Leonard argued in "The Ironies of Partyism and Antipartyism: Origins of Partisan Political Culture in Jacksonian Illinois" that antipartyism was not only widespread in the period but was also interwoven into the very fabric of mainstream political culture.[21]

On this topic, see also Ronald P. Formisano, "Political Character, Antipartyism, and the Second Party System," and Formisano, *For the People: American Populist Movements from the Revolution to the 1850s*.[22] Other important studies of third-party politics include Michael F. Holt's "The Anti-Masonic and Know Nothing Parties" and *Political Parties and American Political Development: From the Age of Jackson to the Age of Lincoln*, Mark Voss-Hubbard's *Beyond Party: Cultures of Antipartisanship in Northern Politics before the Civil War*, and Tyler Anbinder's *Nativism and Slavery: The Northern Know Nothings and the Politics of the 1850s*.[23]

Several excellent studies of state and local politics have extended our understanding of the Jacksonian era. Lee Benson's seminal look at New York and Ronald P. Formisano's account of Michigan politics have already been cited. Benson's work should be supplemented with Sean Wilentz's *Chants Democratic: New York City and the Rise of the American Working Class, 1788-1850* and Reeve Huston's *Land and Freedom: Rural Society, Popular Protest, and Party Politics in Antebellum New York*.[24] Donald Cole, who has written extensively on the period, examined a New England state in *Jacksonian Democracy in New Hampshire, 1800-1851*, while Andrew R. L. Cayton, *The Frontier Republic: Ideology and Politics in the Ohio Country, 1780-1825*; Donald J. Ratcliffe, *The Politics of Long Division: The Birth of the Second Party System in Ohio, 1818-1828*; and Gerald Leonard, *The Invention of Party Politics: Federalism, Popular Sovereignty, and Constitutional Developments in Jacksonian Illinois* explored the Midwest.[25] Southern studies include J. Mills Thornton III's *Politics and Power in a Slave Society: Alabama, 1800-1860*; Marc W. Kruman's *Parties and Politics in North Carolina, 1836-1865*; Harry Watson's previously cited study of local politics in North Carolina; and Jonathan M. Atkins's *Parties, Politics, and the Sectional Conflict in Tennessee, 1832-1861*.[26] Two studies of the influential state of Virginia deserve special attention. William G. Shade claimed that the Old Dominion was typical in the ways it came to accept party politics and the changes that the two-party system brought to the state in *Democratizing the Old Dominion: Virginia and the Second Party System, 1824-1861*.[27] Daniel W. Crofts offered a nuanced portrait of the intertwined nature of social and political activities in a southern community in *Old Southampton: Politics and Society in a Virginia County, 1834-1869.*[28]

The market revolution that led Americans to recalibrate their republican beliefs has been thoroughly explored since the publication in the early 1990s of Harry Watson, *Liberty and Power: The Politics of Jacksonian America,* and Charles Sellers, *The Market Revolution: Jacksonian America, 1815-1846.*[29] Watson skillfully combined the emerging scholarship on the market revolution with the republican interpretation of the period to produce a highly readable general survey of the period. The Democrats and Whigs grew "out of a contest over the relationship between the emerging capitalist economy and the traditions of republican liberty and equality." While it remained difficult to determine why voters chose one party over the other, the Whigs seemed to hold more appeal in areas where the market economy was emerging or established while the Democrats attracted voters in areas where a traditional economy persisted. Watson insisted that the debate over the future of the nation and the nature of American society that framed political discourse in the era was real and that the two parties were substantively different. He also moved Andrew Jackson back to center stage; as a "symbolic leader," Old Hickory shaped the framework within which the great questions of the day were discussed and debated. His administration served as the "catalyst for a rapid transformation of American politics." In dense and jargon-laden prose, Sellers teased out the innumerable ways in which the profound and jarring economic transformations of the era reshaped America. The market revolution dissolved "deeply rooted patterns of behavior and belief" and weakened democracy. Capitalism emerged triumphant and hegemonic; an increasingly bourgeois and Yankeefied middle class held it in place. Andrew Jackson waged a heroic but ultimately unsuccessful battle to defend "patriarchal independence, equality, and . . . honor" against an "activist capitalist state." He turned the epic battle over the Second Bank of the United States into the "acid test of American democracy" by "mobilizing patriarchal democracy against the money power."

Sellers's repeated use of words such as *hegemony, bourgeoisie,* and *exploitative* made clear his political perspective, but *The Market Revolution* stood as the first major synthesis of the period since Schlesinger. And like *The Age of Jackson,* Sellers's work drew criticism and prompted renewed debates about the nature of American politics and society between the War of 1812 and the Mexican-American War. Some of the arguments for and against Sellers appear in the edited volume by Melvin Stokes and Stephen Conway, *The Market Revolution in America: Social, Political and Religious Expressions, 1800-1880.*[30] A fuller response to Sellers came from Daniel Walker Howe in his sprawling survey *What Hath God Wrought: The Transformation of America, 1815-1848.*[31] The title underscores Howe's contention that improved communications, made possible, for example, by the telegraph, proved essential to the market revolution, to the creation of the second party system, and to the numerous reform movements of the period. Throughout the book Howe contrasted the backward and localistic views of the Democrats with the progressive and nationalistic views of the Whigs. If Whig plans for economic modernization had been acted upon, Howe mused, they "might have undercut the appeal of slavery in the upper South and border states." John Quincy Adams, not Jackson, should be held up as the great hero of the age.

Michael Holt maintained that Henry Clay was the most influential figure of the period in his highly detailed *The Rise and Fall of the American Whig Party: Jacksonian Politics and the Onset of the Civil War.*[32] Holt expertly blends local and national politics to reveal how the Whigs came to power. The key to their success was a combination of well-organized local and state organizations, Clay's leadership, and an economic program predicated upon an active government role in the economy. Although the Whigs originated in reaction to Democratic policies and actions, Holt convincingly proved that their political ideology was genuine and coherent and that it resonated with a substantial portion of the electorate. His contention that Clay's election to the presidency might have saved the Union by forestalling the bloody Civil War is less compelling.

The publication of *What Hath God Wrought* and *The Rise and Fall of the American Whig Party* confirmed the reemergence of traditional narrative accounts of the Age of Jackson. Robert V. Remini, perhaps the leading Jacksonian scholar of his day, has published extensively on the key people and events of the era. His three-volume biography of Jackson—*Andrew Jackson and the Course of American Empire, 1767-1821, Andrew Jackson and the Course of American Freedom, 1822-1833*, and *Andrew Jackson and the Course of American Democracy, 1833-1845*—remains essential reading and serves as a potent reminder of the power of well-written narrative history.[33] Remini has also penned biographies of other important political figures from the period, including *Henry Clay: Statesman for the Union* and *John Quincy Adams.*[34] Another fine traditional account of key figures is Merrill D. Peterson's *The Great Triumvirate: Webster, Clay, and Calhoun.*[35] H. W. Brands, *Andrew Jackson: His Life and Times,* and Sean Wilentz, *Andrew Jackson: The Seventh President, 1829-1837,* offer balanced assessments of Jackson and attest to the continuing interest in him and in the period that bears his name.[36]

A useful brief survey of the period can be found in Daniel Feller's *The Jacksonian Promise: America, 1815-1840.*[37] Feller emphasized the optimism of the period among all Americans and their unshakeable belief "in their ability to mold and direct their own destiny and that of the world." This promise of a better world defined the period more than the market revolution or party battles. Sean Wilentz shared this optimistic view of the period in his massive *The Rise of American Democracy: Jefferson to Lincoln.*[38] Wide-ranging, deeply researched, and engagingly written, Wilentz's work stands with Schlesinger's and Sellers's as the most important interpretations of the Jacksonian period. Wilentz successfully integrated the themes that have shaped writings on the period over the last sixty years—the traditional focus on Jackson and bitter partisan debates, the new political history, the social and cultural history of the 1960s and 1970s, republicanism, and the market revolution—into a master narrative that firmly established just how formative and critical this period was in the development of American society, politics, and economics. The historians who have researched and written about the era since the publication of Schlesinger's *The Age of Jackson* know this to be the case, although they often disagree about the particulars. A new generation of scholars will undoubtedly extend and amplify the debate over the true nature of politics in the Jacksonian period.

NOTES

1. Arthur M. Schlesinger Jr., *The Age of Jackson* (New York: Little, Brown, 1945).

2. Richard Hofstadter, *The American Political Tradition and the Men Who Made It* (New York: Knopf, 1948).

3. Louis Hartz, *The Liberal Tradition in America: An Interpretation of American Political Thought since the Revolution* (New York: Harcourt, Brace, 1955).

4. Marvin Meyers, *The Jacksonian Persuasion: Politics and Beliefs* (Palo Alto, Calif., Stanford Univ. Press, 1957).

5. Lee Benson, *The Concept of Jacksonian Democracy: New York as a Test Case* (Princeton, N.J.: Princeton Univ. Press, 1961).

6. Ronald P. Formisano, *The Birth of Mass Political Parties: Michigan, 1827-1861* (Princeton, N.J.: Princeton Univ. Press, 1971); Robert Kelley, *The Cultural Pattern of American Politics: The First Century* (New York: Knopf, 1979).

7. William G. Shade, *Banks or No Banks: The Money Issue in Western Politics, 1832-1865* (Detroit: Wayne State Univ. Press, 1972); James Roger Sharp, *The Jacksonians versus the Banks: Politics in the States after the Panic of 1837* (New York: Columbia Univ. Press, 1970).

8. Richard P. McCormick, *The Second American Party System: Party Formation in the Jacksonian Era* (Chapel Hill: Univ. of North Carolina Press, 1966).

9. William Nisbet Chambers and Walter Dean Burnham, eds., *The American Party Systems: Stages of Political Development* (New York: Oxford Univ. Press, 1967).

10. Joel H. Silbey, *The American Political Nation, 1838-1893* (Palo Alto, Calif., Stanford Univ. Press, 1991).

11. Edward Pessen, *Jacksonian America: Society, Personality, and Politics* (Homewood, Ill.: Dorsey Press, 1969); Major L. Wilson, *Space, Time and Freedom: The Quest for National Identity and the Irrepressible Conflict, 1815-1861* (Westport, Conn.: Greenwood Press, 1974).

12. Richard D. Brown, *Modernization: The Transformation of American Life, 1600-1865* (New York: Hill and Wang, 1976).

13. Daniel Walker Howe, *The Political Culture of the American Whigs* (Chicago: Univ. of Chicago Press, 1979).

14. Linda Kerber, *Federalists in Dissent: Ideology and Imagery in Jeffersonian America* (Ithaca, N.Y.: Cornell Univ. Press, 1970); Lance Banning, *The Jeffersonian Persuasion* (Ithaca, N.Y.: Cornell Univ. Press, 1978); Drew McCoy, *The Elusive Republic: Political Economy in Jeffersonian America* (Chapel Hill: Published for the Institute of Early American History and Culture, Williamsburg, Va., by the Univ. of North Carolina Press, 1980).

15. Howe, *Political Culture of the American Whigs;* Harry L. Watson, *Jacksonian Politics and Community Conflict: The Emergence of the Second American Party System in Cumberland County, North Carolina* (Baton Rouge: Louisiana State Univ. Press, 1981); Major Wilson, "Republicanism and the Idea of Party in the Jacksonian Period," *Journal of the Early Republic* 8 (1988): 419-42.

16. Marc W. Kruman, "The Second American Party System and the Transformation of Revolutionary Republicanism," *Journal of the Early Republic* 12 (1992): 509-37.

17. Sean Wilentz, "On Class and Politics in Jacksonian America," *Reviews in American History* 10 (1982): 45-63.

18. Mary P. Ryan, *Women in Public: Between Banners and Ballots, 1825-1880* (Baltimore: Johns Hopkins Univ. Press, 1990); Elizabeth R. Varon, *We Mean to Be Counted: White Women and Politics in Antebellum Virginia* (Chapel Hill: Univ. of North Carolina Press, 1998).

19. Nancy Isenberg, *Sex and Citizenship in Antebellum America* (Chapel Hill: Univ. of North Carolina Press, 1998).

20. Leon Litwack, *North of Slavery: The Negro in the Free States, 1790-1860* (Chicago: Univ. of Chicago Press, 1961); David W. Blight, *Frederick Douglass' Civil War: Keeping Faith in Jubilee* (Baton Rouge: Louisiana State Univ. Press, 1989).

21. Gerald Leonard, "The Ironies of Partyism and Antipartyism: Origins of Partisan Political Culture in Jacksonian Illinois," *Illinois Historical Journal* 87 (Spring 1994): 21-40.

22. Ronald P. Formisano, "Political Character, Antipartyism, and the Second Party System," *American Quarterly* 21 (Winter 1969): 683-709; Formisano, *For the People: American Populist Movements from the Revolution to the 1850s* (Chapel Hill: Univ. of North Carolina Press, 2007).

23. Michael F. Holt, "The Anti-Masonic and Know Nothing Parties," in *History of U.S. Political Parties,* ed. Arthur M. Schlesinger Jr. (New York: Chelsea House, 1973), 1:575-620; Holt, *Political Parties and American Political Development: From the Age of Jackson to the Age of Lincoln* (Baton Rouge: Louisiana State Univ. Press, 1992); Mark Voss-Hubbard, *Beyond Party: Cultures of Antipartisanship in Northern Politics before the Civil War* (Baltimore: Johns Hopkins Univ. Press, 2002); Tyler Anbinder, *Nativism and Slavery: The Northern Know Nothings and the Politics of the 1850s* (New York: Oxford Univ. Press, 1992).

24. Sean Wilentz, *Chants Democratic: New York City and the Rise of the American Working Class, 1788-1850* (New York: Oxford Univ. Press, 1984); Reeve Huston, *Land and Freedom: Rural Society, Popular Protest, and Party Politics in Antebellum New York* (New York: Oxford Univ. Press, 2000).

25. Donald Cole, *Jacksonian Democracy in New Hampshire, 1800-1851* (Cambridge, Mass.: Harvard Univ. Press, 1970); Andrew R. L. Cayton, *The Frontier Republic: Ideology and Politics in the Ohio Country, 1780-1825* (Kent, Ohio: Kent State Univ. Press, 1986); Donald J. Ratcliffe, *The Politics of Long Division: The Birth of the Second Party System in Ohio, 1818-1828* (Columbus: Ohio State Univ. Press, 2000); Gerald Leonard, *The Invention of Party Politics: Federalism, Popular Sovereignty, and Constitutional Developments in Jacksonian Illinois* (Chapel Hill: Univ. of North Carolina Press, 2002).

26. J. Mills Thornton III, *Politics and Power in a Slave Society: Alabama, 1800-1860* (Baton Rouge: Louisiana State Univ. Press, 1978); Marc W. Kruman, *Parties and Politics in North Carolina, 1836-1865* (Baton Rouge: Louisiana State Univ. Press, 1983); Jonathan M. Atkins, *Parties, Politics, and the Sectional Conflict in Tennessee, 1832-1861* (Knoxville: Univ. of Tennessee Press, 1997).

27. William G. Shade, *Democratizing the Old Dominion: Virginia and the Second Party System, 1824-1861* (Charlottesville: Univ. Press of Virginia, 1996).

28. Daniel W. Crofts, *Old Southampton: Politics and Society in a Virginia County, 1834-1869* (Charlottesville: Univ. Press of Virginia, 1992).

29. Harry Watson, *Liberty and Power: The Politics of Jacksonian America* (New York: Hill and Wang, 1990); Charles Sellers, *The Market Revolution: Jacksonian America, 1815-1846* (Oxford: Oxford Univ. Press, 1991).

30. Melvin Stokes and Stephen Conway, eds., *The Market Revolution in America: Social, Political and Religious Expressions, 1800-1880* (Charlottesville: Univ. Press of Virginia, 1996).

31. Daniel Walker Howe, *What Hath God Wrought: The Transformation of America, 1815-1848* (Oxford: Oxford Univ. Press, 2006).

32. Michael Holt, *The Rise and Fall of the American Whig Party: Jacksonian Politics and the Onset of the Civil War* (Oxford: Oxford Univ. Press, 1999).

33. Robert V. Remini, *Andrew Jackson and the Course of American Empire, 1767-1821*, vol. 1 (New York: Harper and Row, 1977); Remini, *Andrew Jackson and the Course of American Freedom, 1822-1833*, vol. 2 (New York: Harper and Row, 1981); Remini, *Andrew Jackson and the Course of American Democracy*, vol. 3 (New York: Harper and Row, 1984).

34. Robert V. Remini, *Henry Clay: Statesman for the Union* (New York: W. W. Norton, 1991); Remini, *John Quincy Adams* (New York: Times Books, 2002).

35. Merrill D. Peterson, *The Great Triumvirate: Webster, Clay, and Calhoun* (New York: Oxford Univ. Press, 1987).

36. H. W. Brands, *Andrew Jackson: His Life and Times* (New York: Doubleday, 2005); Sean Wilentz, *Andrew Jackson: The Seventh President, 1829-1837* (New York: Henry Holt, 2005).

37. Daniel Feller, *The Jacksonian Promise: America, 1815-1840* (Baltimore: Johns Hopkins Univ. Press, 1995).

38. Sean Wilentz, *The Rise of American Democracy: Jefferson to Lincoln* (New York: W. W. Norton, 2005).

CHAPTER FOUR

The South Carolina Nullification Crisis, 1828-1833

A Historiographical Overview

KEVIN M. GANNON

The Nullification Crisis of 1828-33, which saw South Carolina and the federal government come dangerously near armed conflict over the state's refusal to recognize the legality of federal tariff legislation, was the most fully developed confrontation over the nature of federal authority, the Constitution, and union that occurred in the antebellum United States. Yet many historical accounts of the controversy often characterize it solely in terms of the events that either preceded or were subsequent to it. The pioneering monograph in the historiography of the Nullification Crisis, for example, frames it as a "Prelude to Civil War."[1] Other treatments of the controversy see South Carolina's actions as a chapter in the development of the ideology of states' rights that began with the Virginia and Kentucky Resolutions of 1798 and continued through the antebellum era, culminating in the secession of the Southern cotton states in the aftermath of Abraham Lincoln's 1860 election to the presidency. While these characterizations are useful in contextualizing the events of the Nullification Crisis, they tend to somewhat elide its significance by placing it in an almost deterministic framework. Viewing South Carolina's nullification of federal tariff legislation through the lens of the Civil

War, for example, inserts an 1850s–60s style of Southern "nationalism" into the 1830s, obscuring the historically distinct elements of South Carolina's deployment of a particular states' rights ideology. Perceiving the confrontation as merely an extension and elaboration of the debate over the so-called compact theory of the Constitution that flared up in 1798 ignores the important ways in which the terms of that debated had been modified or altered altogether.[2] The challenge facing scholars of the Nullification Crisis, then, has been to elaborate on its place within the larger political culture of the antebellum United States while maintaining a proper emphasis on the distinct and contingent elements of the crisis's particular context.

To briefly summarize, the short-term causes of the Nullification Crisis lay in the federal tariff laws passed in 1828 (the infamous "Tariff of Abominations" in the eyes of its critics) and 1832. These tariffs were controversial in that their explicit purpose was protective; they were (often quite high) taxes levied on certain foreign manufactured goods imported into the United States in order to "protect" the infant domestic manufacturing sector. This protective element gave the tariff legislation distinctively sectional overtones, however. The South, with its staple-crop agricultural economy, was almost exclusively dependent on imported manufactures; southerners argued that a protective tariff drove up the prices of *all* manufactured goods, not just foreign imports, and therefore had a disproportionate economic effect on their section of the country. Southern farmers and planters worried also about the possibility that foreign nations (particularly Great Britain) would retaliate in the form of protective tariffs of their own. Since southern cotton had come to compose more than one-half of all U.S. exports by the 1820s and 1830s, this was no small concern. Overlaying these specific economic concerns, though, were larger issues of sectional comity and constitutional interpretation. Was it right for the federal government to pass legislation that avowedly favored the interests of one section of the Union (in this case, the manufacturing mid-Atlantic and New England states) over the others? Was it fair for one section of the Union (the southern agricultural states) to bear the bulk of the economic burdens associated with the protective tariff? And was the federal government even entitled to pass tariffs for the purpose of protecting domestic manufactures from foreign competition (as opposed to measures designed solely for revenue, which *were* constitutional)? These overarching debates over sectional parity and federal powers were the mechanisms that drove nullification in South Carolina to the point of becoming a full-fledged crisis of the Union.[3]

When Congress passed another protective tariff in 1832, South Carolina acted. The architect of nullification was Vice President John C. Calhoun; he would relinquish that post, however, and move into the Senate, where he spearheaded the nullificationist movement. In November 1832 a special convention called by the state legislature declared the tariffs of 1828 and 1832 unconstitutional and therefore null and void within South Carolina. President Andrew Jackson, despite his own support for states' rights, acted quickly to assert federal authority. He issued a proclamation to South Carolina denouncing nullification and broaching the possibility of forcible execution of federal laws. He asked Congress to pass legislation to empower him to use the military to collect tariff revenue; Congress complied with the Force Act of 1833. Simultaneously, though, cooler heads were working toward compromise. Senators Calhoun and Henry Clay collaborated on a compromise tariff bill that phased out protectionism over the next decade, which Congress passed at nearly the same time as the Force Act. Deciding that this "compromise tariff" was enough of a vindication of South Carolina's principled stand, Calhoun and the nullifiers called another state convention in February 1833, where the previous Ordinance of Nullification was rescinded. But, for good measure, the state nullified the Force Act (somewhat of a moot point at this juncture but an important assertion of principle that was never forcefully repudiated). Each side—Jackson and the nationalists on one and Calhoun and the Nullifiers on the other—was therefore able to claim victory in what had become the most significant clash of federal and state sovereignty up to this point in the republic's brief history.[4]

But this crisis was more complex, and the issues more intricate and essential, than a brief synopsis suggests. The historiography of the Nullification Crisis is distinguished by its careful—even microscopic—focus on particular elements of the crisis, ranging from the economic to the ideological to the racial. One of the most immediately apparent questions is, why South Carolina? What was it about that state—alone among the slave states—that created the conditions for nullification? William Freehling and James M. Banner Jr. have pointed out that South Carolina, among all of the slave states, felt its position to be the most precarious and thus reacted the most strongly to what it saw as the serious economic and constitutional threats posed by protective tariff legislation. In its low-country districts, the black to white population ratio could reach as high as ten to one because of the armies of slave laborers on the swampy rice plantations of the coast. To a slave-owning class sensitive to threats from within, this imbalance was a source of considerable anxiety, especially in the wake of the Denmark Vesey rebellion scare in 1822 and an invigorated and militant abolitionist movement that had made significant waves by the early 1830s. The state was also hemorrhaging people; emigration from South Carolina had intensified throughout the 1820s as repeated cotton harvests depleted the soil and Carolinians looked westward to restart their planting ventures in a more profitable environment.[5]

These socioeconomic and demographic anxieties, the Banner-Freehling argument concludes, created the environment in which South Carolina's unique political culture, one that ran so counter to the general trends of "Jacksonian democracy," was able to flourish. For Freehling, South Carolina's profound anxieties were the result of the conditions of the slave society that had evolved in the state. The planter elite was acutely sensitive to any threat to the stability (however real or imagined) of slavery; thus the government that could move beyond its constitutional bounds with a protective tariff might also do so concerning slavery, should the precedent be allowed to stand.[6] In Banner's estimation, the "problem" was that "South Carolina, the last refuge of the anti-party tradition, would not govern itself by the political code of the rest of the nation." Thus, "not the challenge of opposition, but only the threat of force, coupled with a timely tariff compromise, could discipline the nullifiers." This was because "the transfer from personal to institutionalized power so necessary to party government had not occurred there."[7] For more than two decades, this interpretation—South Carolina exceptionalism, in essence—held sway.

But it has been challenged, and largely successfully, by closer and more nuanced studies of South Carolinian political culture. The system of personal, no-party politics at the root of Banner's interpretation was more complicated than Banner estimated, for example; John C. Calhoun towered over the state's politics, but he did not do so unchallenged. Organized political factions did exist in the state, and the contours of Jacksonian politics were evident as well, albeit in a somewhat modified form. "The difference between Jacksonian politics in South Carolina and elsewhere in the South," observes Lacy Ford, "lay chiefly in the perception of most South Carolinians that the forces working to undermine republican values were operating only in Washington, or at least beyond the borders of South Carolina, while other Southern states usually found a number of hostile forces at work within their own borders."[8] While the demographics, economic strains, and fears surrounding the security of slavery were important factors behind South Carolina's moving further than any other state to embrace nullification, Ford argues, they were not *exclusive* factors. Rather, "a striking confluence of idiosyncrasies pushed South Carolina toward radical protest against high tariffs," and it was their "collective influence . . . rather than the overwhelming influence of any single factor" that created the climate for nullification: "The special vulnerability of South Carolina to the fluctuations of the world cotton economy and to competition from other cotton regions, the high incidence of slaveholding in the state, the size of the black majority in the Lowcountry, the state's unique political heritage, and the presence of John C. Calhoun were each necessary, but insufficient, conditions for nullification. Each factor contributed in some way toward making nullification possible, but it was the collective force of them all operating together that made nullification a reality in South Carolina." Conversely, "it was the absence of this particular confluence of forces in other states that made it unlikely that the rest of the South would join" the state in nullifying federal tariff legislation. "South Carolina did not nullify alone because her fears were unique," Ford concludes, "but because her circumstances were exceptional."[9]

This question of how "alone" South Carolina's nullifiers were in their course is a crucial one. Antitariff sentiment was prevalent throughout the South, as protectionism was widely viewed as detrimental to the region's economic health and to sectional parity. In fact, a look beyond the official reactions emanating solely from state legislatures to South Carolina's proclamation reveals that the Carolinians were not as isolated as conventional historiographic wisdom once held. Indeed, substantial sympathy and expressions of support for their actions could be found throughout various sectors of slave-state opinion. Richard Ellis, for example, discerns in Georgia and Virginia important sectors of support for South Carolina's nullifiers. In Georgia, there was "an active and articulate minority" that favored unity with South Carolina (strengthening this faction was the ongoing debate over sovereignty between Georgia and the federal government over Cherokee lands). While many adherents of states' rights and the compact theory of constitutional interpretation in Georgia were initially chary of South Carolina's position, Jackson's December proclamation altered the dynamics substantially, according to Ellis. "Focusing on the Proclamation," he argues, allowed pronullification Georgians "to successfully shift attention away from the question of whether or not nullification was a proper constitutional and legal remedy and onto the dangers involved in allowing the President to use the powers of the federal government to coerce a single state."[10] In Virginia, Ellis also finds evidence of significant pockets of support for nullification as well as a shift toward a more favorable perception of South Carolina's stance as a reaction to the forceful nationalism of Jackson's proclamation. Governor John Floyd was an explicit and vocal supporter of nullification, as were several other prominent Virginians. Shortly after Jackson issued his proclamation, the state's legislature approved a committee report that endorsed the compact theory of the Constitution and approved nullification in the abstract, though it stopped short of explicitly endorsing South Carolina's particular use of the doctrine. Ellis contends that this reluctance of the legislature to move more openly in support of South Carolina was not evidence of a weak pronullification faction in the state. Indeed, he argues, the primary effect of Jackson's proclamation was to underscore the states' rights bona fides of Floyd and the pro-Nullifiers, who "were more convinced than ever that Jackson's enormous popularity as well as his willingness to use all the authority of the President's office, even to the point of exceeding his authority, made him dangerous, and that he had to be opposed and restrained at all costs." Thus a powerful states' rights faction emerged in Virginia that would become a powerful component of the state's political culture.[11]

Ellis's emphasis on the reaction to Jackson's proclamation of December 1832 resonates with David Ericson's study of the Force Bill debates of January and February 1833, in that both studies perform the salutary task of highlighting the importance of contingency in shaping the development of the Nullification Crisis. Ericson argues, for example, that three different—though mutually informed by one another—dialects emerged from the common wellspring of American republicanism. Revealed in the Force Bill debates, he continues, were a "federal-republican bloc" that hewed to a states' rights/compact theory interpretation of the Union, a "national-republican bloc" that saw the union as nationally sovereign, and a "centrist bloc" that mediated between these two positions by emphasizing the "partly federal, partly national" and therefore "compound nature of the American republic."[12] Ultimately, Ericson concludes, the centrist strand of this argument emerged triumphant (albeit temporarily) out of the Nullification Crisis, as it seemed to speak most immediately to the Republic's character at that precise moment—and it also proved the most amenable to the compromise options (including the 1833 tariff) then on the table.

Of course, any assessment of the origins and outcomes of the Nullification Crisis involves, to a significant degree, coming to terms with the motivations and thoughts of John C. Calhoun—the intellectual godfather of nullification and principal antagonist of Andrew Jackson. What infuriated Jackson and his supporters during the Nullification Crisis was in part the same issue that has engaged the attention of subsequent scholars: how to assess Calhoun's astounding ideological transformation from arch-nationalist to the architect of nullification in less than twenty years. Though many suspected Calhoun as the author of the 1828 *Exposition,* this was not publicly confirmed until 1831, in Calhoun's "Fort Hill Address." Why did Calhoun abandon the vigorous nationalism of his early public career in favor of its opposite? One of Calhoun's early scholarly biographers asserts that Calhoun was pushed into nullification through principle; it was a "safety valve" to ease the pressures of secessionism in South Carolina's "war against the tariff." Calhoun, argues Margaret Coit, was in a precarious position—his authorship of the exposition was an open secret, and his reluctance to overtly avow nullification was thus "a black mark against him." Having lost his national influence through his falling out with Andrew Jackson, Calhoun had hoped to use nullification as a "double-edged weapon, as a last hope for the South and as a threat to the North, compelling surrender on southern terms" in the controversy over protectionism and sectional parity.[13] Not all scholars would agree with Coit's generous assessment of Calhoun's motives. In his tellingly titled study *John C. Calhoun: Opportunist,* Gerald M. Capers characterized Calhoun's political transformation in terms of the more base motives of partisanship. Calhoun was being outflanked in his home state by the Radical Party, a group of extreme states' rights politicians led by his nemesis, William Smith. The 1828 tariff had given the Radicals significant political capital, and Calhoun faced the unpleasant task of protecting his presidential ambitions nationally while maintaining his South Carolina base; as for the Radicals, Capers argues, Calhoun "probably . . . was actually busy trying to retard and at the same time to catch up with them." For Capers, Calhoun's early nationalism had been based on a more sanguine view of public virtue than the reality of the current tariff debates allowed for. In creating a foundation for vigorous nationalism in federal policy in his early career, Calhoun "now found himself in the disturbing dilemma of having worked half his life to create what turned out to be a Frankenstein's monster." Capers's assessment of Calhoun's efforts to abandon his early position and save political face in the changing climate of his home state is blunt: "It is foolish to regard him, despite the dispassionate language of his "Exposition," as a political scientist abstractly theorizing about the nature of the Union. *With him political considerations were foremost,* for *his* own fate and that of his America and *his* South were at stake."[14] The question thus becomes where Calhoun fell on the spectrum bounded by pure principle on one hand and naked ambition on the other.

More nuanced explanations are found in John Niven's study of Calhoun, which finds a significant degree of consistency in Calhoun's thought, though tempered and adjusted to a Union undergoing the dizzying territorial and economic expansion of the 1820s. These conditions dictated what was, in Niven's view, a defensive tone within the *Exposition,* "reflecting Calhoun's sense of personal isolation and alienation from what the Union of his youth and young manhood had become." "Repeatedly he underscored," Niven continues, "the growing weakness of his state and his region . . . at the mercy, as he saw it, of outside sources . . . that were surely reducing his state and region to a colonial status." In this view, Calhoun reflected the siege mentality that had come to color South Carolina's relations with the federal government by the latter half of the 1820s. Pauline Maier reinforces Niven's assertions of consistency in Calhoun's thought in her observation that for Calhoun (and others), nullification grew naturally out of the ideology of the revolutionary era. "The doctrine's widespread appeal," Maier contends, "confirms its cogency to a generation of Americans fully emersed [*sic*] in the revolutionary and constitutional tradition of the Anglo-American world, where power evoked not hope, but fear, and who considered the division of authority between state and nation a critical safeguard of their freedom." In this vein, then, Calhoun can be more properly seen as "the last of the founding fathers, the last of a generation of creative constitutional statesmen."[15] "Judging

Calhoun's thought from this viewpoint, which in some respects foreshadows the agrarian populism of a later day, and in other respects an extension of the original intent of the founding fathers," according to Niven, "one sees that his understanding of a national union based upon reciprocal interests had never changed."[16]

The problem, however, is that the actual Union *had* changed; Calhoun's vision of some idealized Athenian polis where interests were respectful of one another and where idealism and devotion to the commonweal reigned in the public mind was probably never an accurate reflection of the polity in which he lived. Thus Niven's argument for basic consistency ought to be read against that of Lacy Ford, who suggests that Calhoun was painfully aware of this disconnect between ideal and reality and that the remedy for this went against the grain of one of the most important strands of the founders' thought. James Madison had argued "that the Constitution had divided sovereignty and vested an essential portion of it in the American or national people," as opposed to the states themselves, as Calhoun's articulation of the compact theory claimed. Thus, "on crucial points, Calhoun's republican theory stood the Madisonian legacy on its head," according to Ford. "Madison's contention that a multiplicity of factions and a large territory would inoculate the new American republic against the disease of majoritarianism" was belied by the circumstances of Calhoun's own time and its phenomenon of Jacksonian democracy. "By 1832 Calhoun confronted what he perceived as a dangerously powerful national government supported by a dangerously democratic national majority," Ford asserts; therefore, "in a decidedly nationalistic age, Calhoun strove to revive local power."[17]

Ultimately, this effort at revival proved successful in at least one significant respect: nullification was "defeated" in 1833 but not delegitimized. At the time, however, this element of long-term importance was not immediately apparent to Carolinians facing what they saw as increasing federal and abolitionist pressure against the political economy and institutions of their section. By 1842, even the compromise that had ended the crisis was invalidated as Congress revised tariff legislation to effectively invalidate the injunction of the 1833 tariff to phase out protectionism by 1843. The Panic of 1837 changed the timetable for protectionism and re-kindled the enthusiasm of its advocates. This repudiation of the 1833 compromise, and the inability of South Carolina to stand in its way, is proof for some scholars of the essential "hollowness of South Carolina's supposed victory" in 1833. No other state supported South Carolina in its course, this argument continues, and "the crisis provoked nationalists of various kinds to make assertions of federal power . . . and to establish precedents such as the Force Act . . . that were the very antithesis of what the nullifiers wanted."[18] While this view may accurately describe the immediate consensus that emerged out of the Nullification Crisis, in reality the "resolution" of the episode was more complex and ambiguous to the degree that almost belies that term. In the long run, the ideological construct of the nullifiers—especially Calhoun—remained intact. As Richard Ellis observes, this "seemingly inconclusive outcome . . . should not obscure the fact that it basically worked to the advantage of the nullifiers." South Carolina "succeeded in nullifying the Force Act, and was not required to recant on any aspect of its controversial theory of the nature of the Union."[19] Indeed, one of the most salient points for scholars of this period to apprehend is that temporary repudiation did not equal meaningful recantation. As the historiography of the subject demonstrates, the Nullification Crisis was more than a benchmark moment as one looked ahead to the coming of the Civil War; it involved vitally important strands of political, economic, and constitutional discourse that in many ways culminated in this crisis of the early 1830s. Historians of this period thus continue to fashion a scholarly conversation that is mindful of both distinctions among and connections with and between South Carolina's challenge to federal sovereignty and the larger political culture of the antebellum republic.

NOTES

1. William Freehling, *Prelude to Civil War: The Nullification Controversy in South Carolina, 1816-1836* (New York: Oxford Univ. Press, 1965).

2. This is also the argument made by David F. Ericson, "The Nullification Crisis, American Republicanism, and the Force Bill Debate," *Journal of Southern History* 61 (May 1995): 249-70, esp. 249-52.

3. Good general summaries of the economic and ideological debates at the root of the Nullification Crisis may be found in Freehling, *Prelude to Civil War,* 116-59; Richard E. Ellis, *The Union at Risk: Jacksonian Democracy, States' Rights and the Nullification Crisis* (New York: Oxford Univ. Press, 1987), 41-73; Harry L. Watson, *Liberty and Power: The Politics of Jacksonian America,* 2nd ed. (New York: Hill and Wang, 2006), 113-31; Daniel Walker Howe, *What Hath God Wrought: The Transformation of America, 1815-1848* (New York: Oxford Univ. Press, 2007), 367-73, 395-410. The best summary of the origins of the Nullification Crisis in South Carolina itself is Lacy K. Ford Jr., *Origins of Southern Radicalism: The South Carolina Upcountry, 1800-1860* (New York: Oxford Univ. Press, 1988), 99-144.

4. Concise synopses of these events may be found in Howe, *What Hath God Wrought;* Freehling, *Prelude to Civil War,* 260-97; and Glyndon G. Van Deusen, *The Jacksonian Era, 1828-1848* (New York: Harper and Brothers, 1959), 70-81.

5. Freehling, *Prelude to Civil War,* esp. 7-86; James M. Banner Jr., "The Problem of South Carolina," in *The Hofstadter Aegis: A Memorial,* ed. Stanley Elkins and Eric McKitrick (New York: Alfred A. Knopf, 1974), 60-93, esp. 66-69.

6. A succinct summary of Freehling's argument can be found in *Prelude to Civil War,* 359-60; he explores what he sees as the direct relationship between nullification and the defense of slavery in ibid., 301-60.

7. Banner, "Problem of South Carolina," 92-93. Banner here invokes Freehling's similar arguments about South Carolina's social and political dynamics; see Freehling, *Prelude to Civil War,* 19-24.

8. Ford, *Origins of Southern Radicalism,* 143.

9. Ibid., 121, 124.

10. Ellis, *Union at Risk,* 109-10.

11. Ibid., 123-40, quoted at 139.

12. Ericson, "Nullification Crisis," 249-52 (quoted at 252). Also see Ericson's expansion of this article's themes in his *The Shaping of American Liberalism: The Debates over Ratification, Nullification, and Slavery* (Chicago: Univ. of Chicago Press, 1993), 75-113.

13. Margaret L. Coit, *John C. Calhoun: American Portrait,* Southern Classics Series (1950; Columbia: Univ. of South Carolina Press, 1991), 226-41, quoted at 230.

14. Gerald M. Capers, *John C. Calhoun: Opportunist* (Chicago: Quadrangle Books, 1969), 106-9 (emphasis added).

15. John Niven, *John C. Calhoun and the Price of Union* (Baton Rouge: Louisiana State Univ. Press, 1988), 161-62; Pauline Maier, "The Road Not Taken: Nullification, John C. Calhoun, and the Revolutionary Tradition in South Carolina," *South Carolina Historical Magazine* 82 (1981): 1-19, quoted at 14-15. Maier here is disputing the contention of the "progressive historians" of earlier decades, who argued that states' rights ideology was merely a cover for a particular southern economic agenda and was more an instrument of convenience than an authentic part of political culture. The representative example of this argument is Arthur M. Schlesinger, "The States' Rights Fetish," in *New Viewpoints in American History* (New York: Macmillan, 1922), 220-44.

16. Niven, *John C. Calhoun and the Price of Union,* 161-62, see also xv-xvi.

17. Lacy K. Ford Jr., "Inventing the Concurrent Majority: Madison, Calhoun, and the Problem of Majoritarianism in American Political Thought," *Journal of Southern History* 60 (Feb. 1994): 19-58, quoted at 48, 49, 51. See also Ford, "Republican Ideology in a Slave Society: The Political Economy of John C. Calhoun," *Journal of Southern History* 54 (Aug. 1988): 405-24.

18. This is the conclusion of one of the most recent scholarly treatments of nullification. Donald Ratcliffe, "The Nullification Crisis, Southern Discontents, and the American Political Process," *American Nineteenth Century History* 1 (2000): 1-30, quoted at 21, 22.

19. Ellis, *Union at Risk,* 183, 180.

CHAPTER FIVE

Seeking the Mainstream

The Historiography of Indian Removal

JOHN T. ELLISOR

During the whole of the nineteenth century, historians showed little or no interest in exploring Indian removal, despite the fact that Andrew Jackson considered it the most difficult of his presidential duties, and numerous congressmen serving with him thought it the most important question they faced. Guided by Manifest Destiny and social Darwinism, nineteenth-century historians simply saw no need to discuss Indian removal any more than they would the cutting of forests or the killing of wild beasts, all mundane events as Americans cleared the natural environment to build a nation. But with the dawning of the twentieth century, a few scattered rays of light fell on the dusty removal records. Frederick Jackson Turner heralded the closing of the American frontier and contended that the frontier had been a key element in the development of American democracy. Consequently, more historians became interested in studying the frontier and events related to it, including Indian affairs. At that point, the first book-length publications involving Indian removal appeared, the most important being Annie Heloise Abel's *The History of Events Resulting in Indian Consolidation West of the Mississippi*.[1]

Yet, despite Abel's excellent beginning, historians for the most part remained uninterested in Indian removal. Then came Grant Foreman, an Oklahoma lawyer. He published *Indian Removal:*

The Emigration of the Five Civilized Tribes, which, despite its age and some flaws, remains one of the best single volumes on the emigration of the southern Indians.[2] Foreman followed that book with another devoted to the removal experience of the northern tribes, *The Last Trek of the Indians.*[3]

Undoubtedly, Foreman's books sensitized many Americans to the injustices of Indian removal, but few were convinced of its historical significance. As proof of this fact, one need look only so far as Arthur M. Schlesinger Jr.'s famous work, *The Age of Jackson,* published in 1945. This book, considered a must-read for all self-respecting American historians, says nothing about Indian removal. Representing the view of many of his contemporary academicians, Schlesinger did not consider Jackson's Indian policy in any way crucial to understanding Jacksonian democracy. Nor, it would be safe to say, did these scholars see Indian removal as a major event in the nation's history. Natives and their misfortunes still stood outside the mainstream of American history and historiography.[4]

Such was the case throughout the 1950s, that decade of consensus history when so many scholars sought to highlight all the good things Americans held in common and to glorify the great national achievements. Indian removal did not fit the paradigm, so historians continued to neglect it as a topic of study. But, fortunately, things changed with the coming of the tumultuous 1960s. During that decade, blacks, Natives, women, and others pushed for full equality in American society. Simultaneously, a great youth movement challenged the nation's stifling conservatism and destructive militarism. In the midst of all this, historians tended to become more liberal, even radical, and take a greater interest in the histories of America's subaltern groups. In fact, the 1960s gave birth to Native American history as a distinct discipline, and, not surprisingly, works on Indian removal began to appear in greater abundance.

Mary E. Young kicked off the new era in removal historiography with her book *Redskins, Ruffleshirts and Rednecks: Indian Allotments in Alabama and Mississippi, 1830-1860.* This book's significance lies in the fact that it shows how important Indian policy was in defining what Jacksonian democracy really meant. After all, that democracy depended on economic opportunity in the form of territorial expansion, and that expansion depended on acquiring Indian land. In Alabama and Mississippi, that acquisition depended in turn on the Indian allotment system, a process whereby the government divided the Native lands out to individual families in severalty and allowed them to sell or retain those allotments as they saw fit. This seemingly democratic and fair system, which seemed to respect Native property and contract rights, then allowed the Jackson administration to use the tender mercies of the marketplace to coerce the Indians into removal. Speculators moved in to cheat the Indians out of their lands and leave them no choice but to emigrate beyond the Mississippi. Thus Young shows how an aggressive, free-for-all acquisitiveness lay at the heart of Jacksonian democracy and how men claiming a commitment to justice and equality of opportunity in a democratic society could actually use those high ideals as a cover for the pursuit of wealth at the expense of others.[5]

Other historians writing in the 1960s chose to look at the removal experience of the Cherokees, particularly their efforts to have the Supreme Court recognize their sovereign rights as a nation against the state of Georgia. These historians believed that the failure of the Cherokees to have those rights recognized and protected by the federal government ultimately led not only to Cherokee removal but also to the emigration of all the other southern Natives. One of these scholars, Allen Guttman, produced *States' Rights and Indian Removal: The Cherokee Nation versus the State of Georgia*.[6] A few years later, Joseph C. Burke published a particularly important study titled "The Cherokee Cases: A Study in Law, Politics, and Morality." Burke's article is significant because it wove the removal issue tightly into the fascinating world of Jacksonian politics. Indeed, Burke shows how John Marshall and his fellow justices of the Supreme Court, after first deciding against the extension of Georgia's laws over the Cherokees (*Worcester v. Georgia*) and thereby upholding Cherokee sovereignty, ultimately turned a blind eye to Cherokee rights to stand firmly behind President Jackson against South Carolina in the nullification controversy. For Marshall and his cohorts, preserving the power of the court and defending the principles of union and strong central government were more important than Cherokee sovereignty. In recent years, however, other historians and legal scholars have added their own interpretations of the Cherokee cases, and, undoubtedly, those cases will continue as a major area of interest within removal historiography.[7]

Historians writing in the 1960s also added other interesting angles to the removal story. John K. Mahon, for example, wrote his *History of the Second Seminole War, 1835-1842* to show how the United States waged an extensive military campaign to remove the Seminoles from Florida.[8] For his part, Bert Anson, in an article titled "Variations of the Indian Conflict: The Effects of the Emigrant Indian Removal Policy, 1830-1854," shows how the movement of eastern Indians into the trans-Mississippi prairies and plains had a negative impact on the western tribes. The immigrants intruded on the hunting grounds of the westerners, used arms acquired from whites to best the westerners in fights, and passed on to them vices acquired from the whites. Thus Anson revealed that Indian removal, though targeting the eastern tribes, sent negative shock waves through all Native American tribes. This was an ironic situation given Jackson's promise that removal would serve to preserve Indian culture.[9]

But the historians of the 1960s discovered other ironies in Indian removal. Dale Van Every, author of *Disinherited: The Lost Birthright of the American Indian,* found that, while most northerners disapproved of Indian removal, their congressmen, both Whig and Democrat, voted in favor of removal in order to appease proremoval southerners and keep the two parties unified in their contest for political power against one another. Moreover, northerners were willing to lay aside their moral objections to removal in order to realize the economic opportunity that clearing the land of Indians would bring. And, finally, Van Every points out that because the North experienced so much immigration from foreign lands, northern people saw life as a constant competition between ethnic groups, and this made it easier for them, indeed inclined them to overlook their moral scruples and take advantage of the Native Americans as part of that larger culture of competition. Thus an ironic miscarriage of justice occurred as a consequence of some of the very strengths of American democracy: the freedom of economic enterprise, the two-party system, the concept of the country as a haven for refugees from all parts, and, of course, the division of power between state and federal governments, which, while promoting the freedom of citizens, also allowed some of those same citizens, working through state governments, to pressure their Indian populations into moving west.[10]

The 1960s also gave rise to the first piece of controversy in the writing of removal history. Francis Paul Prucha, the leading authority on United States–Indian relations, took exception to the fact that Van Every and other liberal historians, generally the authors of the textbooks of the time, had adopted what Prucha called a "devil theory" of American Indian policy, always portraying the federal government as a ruthless villain in terms of its treatment of the Natives. In particular, Prucha objected to what he believed was their unfair depiction of Andrew Jackson as a frontier bully and Indian hater who forced the Indians west at gunpoint. In "Andrew Jackson's Indian Policy: A Reassessment," Prucha defended Jackson against his critics and, by extension, defended his entire removal program. Basically, Prucha said, Jackson did not hate Indians and advocated removal for a number of good reasons, such as protecting national security, promoting economic development, and protecting Indians and their culture from the destructive influences of white civilization. Furthermore, argued Prucha, Jackson had no choice but to remove the Indians, given the nature of the times. Sending large numbers of troops to the states to keep the peace and protect the Indians from aggressive speculators and settlers was the only other alternative, and realistically no president could do that effectively.[11]

One of main removal texts of the 1970s generally followed Prucha's line of reasoning. Ronald N. Satz, author of *American Indian Policy in the Jacksonian Era,* contended that the plan was generally popular throughout the nation and that removal was reasonable for all the reasons Prucha had previously outlined. In fact, removal, when presented by Jackson and others in humanitarian terms, actually appealed to many Americans as a very Christian and enlightened policy. Furthermore, Satz claimed that those politicians who objected to removal did not do so out of any heartfelt sympathy for the Natives. Henry Clay and the other members of the nascent Whig Party merely used Jackson's removal bill and their opposition to it as a political football, hoping to latch on to an issue that would cause the Democrats problems. Then, when the Whigs finally gained real power in the government, they actually continued their former enemy's removal policy unabated, leading Satz to conclude that the United States in the Jacksonian era was a market-driven society dominated by capitalists intent on removing all obstacles to exploitation of natural resources, including Indians, and therefore that no political party could really stand up for the Natives and survive. Nevertheless, Satz did note Jackson's coercive measures to bring removal about and did criticize removal as a failure, owing not to Jackson's intent but to bad planning, bureaucratic incompetence, lack of funds, disease, foul weather, the greed of removal contractors, and the aggressiveness of land speculators and settlers, all of which caused the Indians much suffering.[12]

However, the other major removal texts of the 1970s did not go quite so easy on Jackson. In *The Removal of the Choctaw Indians,* Arthur H. DeRosier Jr. claimed that Jackson, unlike previous presidents, had threatened the Choctaws with the armed might of the United States if they did not vacate their ancient homeland. Furthermore, Jackson's minions used the Choctaw removal as a test case, developing techniques, including threats of violence, that they would use again in all the Native relocations to follow.[13] Similarly, Cecil Eby blamed Jackson, albeit a little more indirectly, for the climate of violence that pervaded Indian removal and resulted in three significant Indian wars, one with the Creeks, another with the Seminoles, and a third with the Sauk and Fox under Chief Black Hawk. Eby produced a book on the Sauk and Fox conflict titled *"That Disgraceful Affair": The Black Hawk War,* and in it attributed blame for the affair squarely at brutish frontiersmen egged on by

Jacksonian democracy. According to Eby, "the milieu of Jackson encouraged the people's power in its most volatile form," including their power to abuse Indians and drive them off Native lands.[14]

Michael Paul Rogin, also writing in the 1970s, gave a much more involved explanation of Jacksonian violence against Indians. In his psychohistory *Fathers and Children: Andrew Jackson and the Subjugation of the American Indian,* he explained that Andrew Jackson and many other white Americans of the time suffered separation anxiety. The nation was growing, modernizing, and becoming more competitive, and old patterns of family and community relationships were breaking down under the press of the market economy. Lonely, alienated, and frustrated Americans took out their anger and hostility on the Indians. Beyond that, Rogin, using Freudian analysis, found another reason for the mayhem. White Americans, he said, had developed a deep psychological need to conquer nature to prove their worth, to gain economic advantage, and to discipline that regressive kinder, gentler part of themselves that longed for lost childhoods and simpler lives more in harmony with nature. To these conflicted Americans, Indians represented nature as well as the childlike parts of themselves they needed to suppress in order to be successful in a liberal society. The result was that these Americans, Andrew Jackson in particular, felt compelled to conquer, discipline, and establish paternal authority over the Natives. Furthermore, said Rogin, the violent subjugation of Natives became the defining characteristic of the time, the very foundation upon which the Age of Jackson rested.[15]

Rogin's provocative book drew a good deal of attention from scholars, but few, if any, followed his lead in using psychology as a tool for interpreting Indian-white relations during the Jacksonian era. Rather, the coming of the 1980s brought forth another defense of Jackson by the man who would establish himself as the leading authority on Old Hickory as both man and politician. Though Robert V. Remini would write much about Jackson and the Natives in other books, he summarized his views on Jackson's removal policy in *The Legacy of Andrew Jackson: Essays on Democracy, Indian Removal, and Slavery.* In this work, Remini claimed that Jackson was not motivated by greed, racism, or genocide in his desire to move Indians west. On the contrary, Jackson believed that Native extinction was imminent without removal. And while Remini admitted that the Indians' resistance to removal caused Jackson to harden his resolve and lose some concern for the Indians' welfare, in the end the president did serve the best interests of the southern tribes by sending them to a place where they ultimately survived and even prospered. Moreover, Remini parceled out some of the blame for the disastrous Cherokee Trail of Tears to John Ross, principal chief of the Cherokee Nation, for resisting removal even when it became inevitable, thus placing his people in harm's way. In the end, Remini admitted that removal caused human misery and death, but he still claimed that Jackson's best intentions motivated him in urging emigration on the Natives.[16]

Remini's views represent a rather conservative, traditional approach to writing about removal; the 1980s, however, are most notable for bringing about a real change in the conceptualization and writing of Native American history in general, and removal history in particular. Prior to that decade, removal studies, for the most part, put whites at the center of the drama. Historians attempted to understand removal from the American point of view or, in Remini's case, Jackson's point of view. More often than not, Indians appeared as the objects of the action; readers saw very little from their perspective. In fact, the Natives continued to appear as they did to nineteenth-century historians, simply parts of the natural landscape, entities without voice being cut down, uprooted, and swept away as so many rocks or trees. But the rise of ethnohistory started to change all that. Using methods drawn from cultural anthropology and other disciplines, some scholars began to write history from the Native point of view. They tried to place Indians in the center of their own history, showing how their distinctive cultures influenced their actions as they attempted to shape their own destinies in the face of American expansionism.[17] Certainly this is what Michael Green tried to do with his book, *The Politics of Indian Removal*. In this pioneering piece of ethnohistory, Green made the Creek National Council the focus of his study and explained the council chiefs' motives and actions as they contested with Georgia, Alabama, and the federal government in a desperate and ultimately unsuccessful attempt to hang on to a piece of their ancient domain and avoid removal to the West.[18]

Beginning early in the 1990s and continuing to the present time, removal studies have increased substantially both in numbers and in the diversity of topics. Some scholars have continued to follow the ethnohistory approach, as illustrated by Dona L. Akers in "Removing the Heart of the Choctaw People: Indian Removal from the Native Perspective." In this interesting article, Akers shows how the Choctaws saw all the misfortunes of removal—death, disease, depression, and so on—as the direct result of leaving an ancient homeland to which they were physically and spiritually attached in ways whites could not comprehend.[19] Similarly, Patrick Minges, author of "Beneath the Underdog: Race, Religion, and the Trail of Tears," contends that Africans, by bringing Christianity to the Creeks and Seminoles and combining it with elements of Native religion, not only established themselves as spiritual leaders among the Indians but also helped create an apocalyptic religious tradition that helps explain the Seminoles' armed resistance to removal.[20]

But Natives also employed other methods to resist or delay removal, and some continued to live in close proximity to whites throughout the Jacksonian era. A few recent studies explore this part of the removal story. Some notable examples are Susan E. Gray's "Limits and Possibilities: White-Indian Relations in Western Michigan in the Era of Removal" and Elizabeth Bollwerk's "Controlling Acculturation: A Potawatomi Strategy for Avoiding Removal."[21]

Recent studies have also done much to enlighten us on the fact that the removal story did not end with the completion of the Trail of Tears. The relocation, or rather dislocation, of Indians continued to affect them negatively for many years, as Jane F. Lancaster writes in *Removal Aftershock: The Seminoles' Struggle to Survive in the West, 1836-1866*.[22]

But still the argument over Andrew Jackson's culpability in removal continues. Alfred A. Cave, in "Abuse of Power: Andrew Jackson and the Indian Removal Act of 1830," makes it clear that the Indian Removal Act of 1830, which Jackson pushed through Congress, stated that Indians would have to agree to removal. Furthermore, the act did not authorize the president to break existing treaties guaranteeing Indians the rights to land in the states where they lived; neither did the act authorize the forced emigration of Indians. But both these things happened because Jackson and his minions resorted to extralegal means to coerce the Natives. Cave goes on to contend that past historians of Indian removal have ignored this disconnect between what the law said and what the president did, which led to the broad misconception and oversimplification that the Removal Act itself was the source of all the misery for the Natives when Jackson alone was largely to blame by misusing the act.[23]

Anthony F. C. Wallace, author of *The Long, Bitter Trail: Andrew Jackson and the Indians,* tends to agree, placing the origin of the removal policy squarely on southern land hunger created by an expanding world cotton market. Furthermore, Wallace shows how Andrew Jackson, a southern planter himself, began his policy of moving Indians off the land long before he became president, using his authority as a military commander and government treaty commissioner to extract land cessions from the Natives. Thus Jackson came to the presidency intent on finally ending Indian occupancy in the Southeast and did in fact do so using extralegal means. Wallace also gives a good account of the removal itself, but he does not stop there, as do many other accounts. He helps flesh out the historical significance of removal by detailing some of its lasting effects on American Indian policy, such as the creation of the Bureau of Indian Affairs, established first to effect Jackson's plans for the Natives and later to administer a myriad of government programs directed in one way or another toward improving Native welfare, just as removal was supposed to have done.[24]

While Cave, and to an extent Wallace, sees Jackson as largely responsible for the excesses of removal, another scholar, Susan M. Ryan, sees the problem as being a societal one, connected to the great reform impulse that distinguished the Jacksonian age. In *The Grammar of Good Intentions: Race and the Antebellum Culture of Benevolence,* Ryan claims that Jacksonian benevolence was merely a tool, a way for white Americans to reconcile the dictates of Christianity with their racism and white superiority. American benevolence was condescending; worse, it was a form of power, another way to subjugate, create dependence in, and control inferior groups of people. Thus some reformers, while advocating Indian removal as a way to save Natives, actually pushed their wards out of the way and even destroyed them with what Ryan calls "benevolent violence."[25]

Mary Hershberger, however, shows the connection between Jacksonian reform and Indian removal in a more positive light. In "Mobilizing Women, Anticipating Abolition: The Struggle against Indian Removal in the 1830s," Hershberger does not show Indian removal as being a popular cause among reformers. On the contrary, she contends that Jackson's plan to remove the southern Indians actually inflamed widespread public opposition in the North, particularly among women, who organized the first women's petition campaign to stop Congress from passing the Indian Removal Act and implementing Jackson's plan. Furthermore, that campaign marked the first entry of organized women's groups into reform politics. In fact, women took the knowledge and experience gained from fighting Indian removal into the other important Jacksonian reform movements, most notably abolitionism.[26]

Whether one agrees with Ryan or Hershberger, their works are important because by connecting removal with the reform theme, they both tend to draw removal back into the mainstream of Jacksonian historiography where it properly belongs. And just as important, a few other scholars have further explored the connection between removal and Jacksonian politics. James Taylor Carson shows us, for example, that in the southern states Indian policy and removal actually helped create a new political faction within the existing party structure. In "State Rights and Indian Removal in Mississippi, 1817-1835," Carson argues that the debate about the extension of state law over Indian land, the cession of Indian land in the state, and the removal of Mississippi's Indians to the West gave rise to a strong states' rights faction that demanded all those things in the name of Mississippi's sovereignty.

And, in this regard, the Indian question actually introduced the states' rights ideology to Mississippi, an ideology that not only altered peoples' thinking on the relationship between the state and the federal government but also ultimately led Mississippi into secession and civil war.[27]

Similarly, Tim Alan Garrison, author of *The Legal Ideology of Removal: The Southern Judiciary and the Sovereignty of Native Americans,* shows how southern removal advocates portrayed removal as a states' rights, as opposed to a moral, issue and used that view to win support for their cause among their fellow southerners as well as win some little-known but very important state supreme court cases. The decisions in these state cases, in turn, enabled states to exert their legal dominion over Indian land and thereby press Natives into emigrating.[28]

John A. Andrews contends that the political battle over Indian removal revealed other ideological differences among Americans, particularly the split between republican and liberal values. In *From Revivals to Removal: Jeremiah Evarts, the Cherokee Nation, and the Search for the Soul of America,* Andrews asserts that Jeremiah Evarts, one of removal's greatest opponents, represented the republican point of view. Evarts saw removal as pure evil, the consequence of the rampant individualism and selfishness overtaking the nation. Unlike Jackson and those liberal Americans who saw individual liberty and unfettered competition as the keys to personal success and national greatness, Evarts stood for those citizens who believed only self-discipline, moral restraint, and public virtue could keep society on track.[29]

Readers can see that the historiography of Indian removal has come a long way, but has all this research and writing really had any sort of telling effect on the American consciousness? Has Indian removal finally entered the mainstream of American historiography? For guidance here, students and scholars should turn to Steven Conn's excellent book, *History's Shadow: Native Americans and Historical Consciousness in the Nineteenth Century.* Conn argues that a sense of cultural superiority caused nineteenth-century intellectuals to remove Indians from the main narrative of American history as well as from their land. Assuming that Natives were an inferior and dying race, these thinkers consigned the study of Indians to the then exotic field of ethnology, not history, and insofar as Francis Parkman and other historians did speak of them, Natives appeared as obstacles Americans had to overcome to reach a higher stage of perfection. Only in the late twentieth century did historians begin to retrieve Native American history, but that retrieval, including removal history, is not yet complete. In fact, Conn declares that Indians remain marginal to the work of most historians, including those writing about the Age of Jackson.[30] This is unfortunate, but perhaps the works mentioned here, along with others not mentioned, including a variety of good doctoral dissertations, which fall outside the purview of this short chapter, will at last make Americans, historians in particular, fully conscious of the importance of Indian removal.

NOTES

1. Annie Heloise Abel, *The History of Events Resulting in Indian Consolidation West of the Mississippi* (Washington, D.C.: American Historical Association, 1908).

2. Grant Foreman, *Indian Removal: The Emigration of the Five Civilized Tribes* (Norman: Univ. of Oklahoma Press, 1932).

3. Grant Foreman, *The Last Trek of the Indians* (Chicago: Univ. of Chicago Press, 1946).

4. Arthur M. Schlesinger Jr., *The Age of Jackson* (New York: Little, Brown, 1945).

5. Mary E. Young, *Redskins, Ruffleshirts and Rednecks: Indian Allotments in Alabama and Mississippi, 1830-1860* (Norman: Univ. of Oklahoma Press, 1961).

6. Allen Guttman, *States' Rights and Indian Removal: The Cherokee Nation versus the State of Georgia* (Washington, D.C.: DC Heath, 1964).

7. Joseph C. Burke, "The Cherokee Cases: A Study in Law, Politics, and Morality," *Stanford Law Review* 21 (Feb. 1969): 500-531.

8. John K. Mahon, *History of the Second Seminole War, 1835-1842* (Gainesville: Univ. of Florida Press, 1967).

9. Bert Anson, "Variations of the Indian Conflict: The Effects of the Emigrant Indian Removal Policy, 1830-1854," *Missouri Historical Review* 59 (Oct. 1964): 64-89.

10. Dale Van Every, *Disinherited: The Lost Birthright of the American Indian* (New York: Morrow and Company, 1966).

11. Francis Paul Prucha, "Andrew Jackson's Indian Policy: A Reassessment," *Journal of American History* 56 (1969): 527-39.

12. Ronald N. Satz, *American Indian Policy in the Jacksonian Era* (Lincoln: Univ. of Nebraska Press, 1975).

13. Arthur H. DeRosier Jr., *The Removal of the Choctaw Indians* (Knoxville: Univ. of Tennessee Press, 1970).

14. Cecil Eby, *"That Disgraceful Affair": The Black Hawk War* (New York: W. W. Norton and Company, 1973), 21.

15. Michael Paul Rogin, *Fathers and Children: Andrew Jackson and the Subjugation of the American Indian* (New York: Knopf, 1975).

16. Robert V. Remini, *The Legacy of Andrew Jackson: Essays on Democracy, Indian Removal, and Slavery* (Baton Rouge: Louisiana State Univ. Press, 1988).

17. Ibid.

18. Michael Green, *The Politics of Indian Removal* (Lincoln: Univ. of Nebraska Press, 1982).

19. Dona L. Akers, "Removing the Heart of the Choctaw People: Indian Removal from the Native Perspective," *American Indian Culture and Research Journal* 23 (Summer 1999): 63-76.

20. Patrick Minges, "Beneath the Underdog: Race, Religion, and the Trail of Tears," *American Indian Quarterly* 25, no. 3 (2001): 453-79.

21. Susan E. Gray, "Limits and Possibilities: White-Indian Relations in Western Michigan in the Era of Removal," *Michigan Historical Review* 20, no. 3 (1994): 71-91; and Elizabeth Bollwerk, "Controlling Acculturation: A Potawatomi Strategy for Avoiding Removal," *Midcontinental Journal of Archaeology* 32, no. 1 (2006): 117-41.

22. Jane F. Lancaster, *Removal Aftershock: The Seminoles' Struggle to Survive in the West, 1836-1866* (Knoxville: Univ. of Tennessee Press, 1994).

23. Alfred A. Cave, "Abuse of Power: Andrew Jackson and the Indian Removal Act of 1830," *Historian* 64, no. 6 (2002): 1330-53.

24. Anthony F. C. Wallace, *The Long, Bitter Trail: Andrew Jackson and the Indians* (New York: Hill and Wang, 1993).

25. Susan M. Ryan, *The Grammar of Good Intentions: Race and the Antebellum Culture of Benevolence* (Ithaca, N.Y.: Cornell Univ. Press, 2005).

26. Mary Hershberger, "Mobilizing Women, Anticipating Abolition: The Struggle against Indian Removal in the 1830s," *Journal of American History* 86 (June 1999): 15-40.

27. James Taylor Carson, "State Rights and Indian Removal in Mississippi, 1817-1835," *Journal of Mississippi History* 57, no. 1 (1995): 25-41.

28. Tim Alan Garrison, *The Legal Ideology of Removal: The Southern Judiciary and the Sovereignty of Native American Nations* (Athens: Univ. of Georgia Press, 2002).

29. John A. Andrews, *From Revivals to Removal: Jeremiah Evarts, the Cherokee Nation, and the Search for the Soul of America* (Athens: Univ. of Georgia Press, 1992).

30. Steven Conn, *History's Shadow: Native Americans and Historical Consciousness in the Nineteenth Century* (Chicago: Univ. of Chicago Press, 2004).

CHAPTER SIX

The Age of Association

Temperance, Antislavery, and Women's Rights Movements
in Jacksonian America

BETH A. SALERNO

On a summer day in July 1848, more than two hundred women and
forty men gathered in a small town in upstate New York near the
Erie Canal. They sat in the Wesleyan Methodist Chapel in Seneca
Falls and listened to a thirty-two-year-old mother of three read a
stirring Declaration of Rights and Sentiments. Elizabeth Cady Stanton had drawn from the example of the Declaration of Independence and proclaimed, "We hold these truths to be self-evident:
that all men *and women* are created equal."[1] For two days the attendees debated the proper extent of women's rights, including the right
to divorce, the right to vote, and access to the professions. On the
last day, more than one hundred people signed their names to the
declaration, and many went on to organize women's rights meet-
ings and organizations across New York, Pennsylvania, and New
England. The effort to win women the right to vote culminated in
1920 with the Nineteenth Amendment to the Constitution.

Historians such as Ellen Carol DuBois and Jean Baker have
seen this meeting in Seneca Falls as the beginning of the women's
suffrage movement or, as one writer put it, "the Lexington and
Concord of the women's 'revolution.'"[2] Yet if one looks backward
rather than forward, it is also clear that the meeting in Seneca Falls
was the end result of a series of political, economic, and social

changes in Jacksonian America. The impact of the market revolution, religious revivals, the expansion of white male suffrage, a communications revolution, debates over slavery, a nationwide fear of moral decline, legal reforms regarding women's property— all these issues came together between 1820 and 1848, particularly along the Erie Canal in upstate New York. These changes brought together people as varied as a working-class glovemaker and an upper-class factory owner's wife, Quakers and Episcopalians, a former slave and antislavery farmers, with the belief that they could and should change their world.

There is hot debate among historians over what to call the period from 1820 to 1848. Daniel Walker Howe's major treatment of the period, *What Hath God Wrought: The Transformation of America, 1815-1848*, avoids the terms "Jacksonian America," "the Age of Jackson," and the "market revolution" in favor of "the Era of the Communications Revolution."[3] Another common term is "antebellum America," used most often by historians focused on the coming of the Civil War. Each term has a different emphasis. An older term, the "Age of Association," best emphasizes the point of this chapter. Drawn from the writings of French political commentator Alexis de Tocqueville, who traveled in America in 1831, the term "Age of Association" highlights the amazing growth and diversity of what are now called unions, brotherhoods, societies, organizations, and political influence groups. De Tocqueville observed that "Americans of all ages, all conditions, all minds constantly unite. Not only do they have commercial and industrial associations in which all take part, but they also have a thousand other kinds . . . ; Americans use associations to give fêtes, to found seminaries, to build inns, to raise churches, to distribute books, to send missionaries to the antipodes; in this manner they create hospitals, prisons, schools."[4] The people in and around Seneca Falls were thoroughly caught up in the association-making process: attendees were members of religious associations, antislavery organizations, and temperance societies. Some women had organized fairs to raise money for antislavery. Others helped to found newspapers to spread the temperance message. Even the

Wesleyan Methodist Chapel itself was a result of association, as a group of churchgoers abandoned their original church in 1843 when the minister refused to allow a woman to speak. They re-organized into a new association and moved to a new building, vowing that it would be open to all speakers, including those proclaiming women's rights.[5]

The women and men attending the Seneca Falls convention, like most people in Jacksonian America, understood that America had a God-given destiny, inherited from the American Revolution. Each individual had a personal responsibility to work toward maintaining and improving that legacy. Yet Americans as a whole disagreed over how exactly to achieve national perfection. This sense of purpose and the political, social, and cultural debates it created are captured in Daniel Feller's study of this period, *The Jacksonian Promise: America, 1815-1840.*[6] Feller portrays a public sphere jam-packed with competing associations. These sometimes used the political system to achieve their ends—to build prisons and poorhouses, to ban alcohol or slavery. But originally they focused their attention not on men's votes but on people's hearts and minds. This chapter focuses on the widespread organized efforts to reduce or eliminate drinking, free the slaves, and change the laws, customs, and beliefs about women's proper roles, as these were the largest and generally most influential reform movements of the period. The temperance, antislavery, and women's rights movements draw together crucial themes of the Jacksonian period.

The temperance movement grew out of an increasing national concern about drunkenness in America. The first scientific evidence of alcohol's negative effects on the body came in 1784.[7] The cost of transporting grain from western farms to eastern cities meant that most farmers distilled grain into whiskey. This dramatically increased the supply and lowered the price of hard liquor, which led to increased drinking and political revolt against excise taxes on liquors (the Whiskey Rebellion of 1794). By the 1830s nearly everyone could afford hard liquor, and the average person was drinking ten gallons a year, more than twice as much as they had in 1790.[8]

People's ability to buy as much liquor as they could drink resulted in part from the market revolution. Historian Charles Sellers framed the current scholarly understanding of this term in *The Market Revolution: Jacksonian America, 1815-1846.* The market revolution was a complex process in which Americans began to participate fully in an international market economy, growing or making goods for far-off customers in exchange for a wage or a cash payment. This economy was subject to booms and busts, and while people could rise high in society on the strength of their hard work and business acumen, they could also fall far due to an accident, bad luck, or, as temperance reformers argued, too much drinking. The middle class, made up of clerks, small businessmen, doctors, and lawyers, began to see temperance, or the moderate use of alcohol, as both a cause and a symbol of their success. Temperance marked their class identity, separating them from the hard-drinking, less successful, and less cultured working class. Over time, these reformers began to portray drinking as a choice that inevitably led to poverty. As one temperance tract noted, "If you are determined to be poor . . . to starve your family . . . to blunt your senses, be a drunkard, and you will soon be more stupid than an ass. . . . You will be dead weight on the community."[9]

These economic changes intersected with and helped to motivate a second crucial change in antebellum America, the Second Great Awakening. Grounded primarily in New England, New York, and the northern Midwest, this series of religious revivals called upon Americans to return to church, save their souls, and engage in benevolent work to reform an increasingly materialistic and immoral American nation. Protestant preachers emphasized how rapid economic and social change had left many people disconnected from family, community, and traditional moral rules. They stressed that greed, corruption, and a lack of focus on moral issues had resulted in a plague of sabbath-breaking, gambling, crime, intemperance, prostitution, religious ignorance, and lack of humanity toward many of God's children, including the poor and the enslaved. Ministers and prominent Protestants founded organizations to spread the message of the Bible, create Sunday schools, and specifically support those groups most likely to be tempted to sin, including the increasing number of young people headed to cities to look for work. Wherever changing economic conditions left anxious groups of people, ministers found fertile ground for revivals. The area around the Erie Canal in upstate New York had so many revivals that historian Whitney R. Cross named it the Burned-over District; we might now call it the Burned-Out District. In some ways one can see the market revolution and the Second Great Awakening as two sides of the same coin. The most dedicated reformers were some of the most active and successful participants in the market revolution. Yet they feared the social and economic disruptions they were creating and sought to use their economic success to mitigate the consequences of rapid economic change. These themes are best explored in Steven Mintz, *Moralists and Modernizers: America's Pre-Civil War Reformers,* and Robert H. Abzug, *Cosmos Crumbling: American Reform and the Religious Imagination.*[10]

The temperance movement, like almost all reform movements of the time, grew out of the intersection of the market revolution and the Second Great Awakening. It became the most widespread and longest lasting reform movement of the nineteenth century and was emblematic of the power of associations to organize people and promote ideas. Although it drew on pre-Revolutionary traditions, it found its Jacksonian voice in 1825. In that year, one of the most prominent Congregational ministers in New England, Lyman Beecher, gave six sermons on temperance attended by hundreds of people. His pamphlet, *Six Sermons on the Nature, Occasions, Signs, Evils, and Remedy of Intemperance,* reached thousands and perhaps millions when it was published in 1827.[11] Inspired by the sermons, dozens of prominent business leaders and clergymen joined Beecher in founding the American Temperance Society in 1826. Within a decade there were temperance associations in hundreds of cities and towns. Each member financially supported the movement, ensuring that newspapers, pamphlets, lectures, and cartoons circulated everywhere, stressing the religious and economic implications of drinking and the real-world impact on lost jobs, abused spouses, and abandoned children.

Until 1837 or so, the temperance movement leadership was predominantly white, male, Protestant, and middle-class. Women made up 35 to 60 percent of the membership of temperance organizations, but they were encouraged to make personal efforts at home—encouraging their husbands, sons, or family friends to temperance—rather than leading organizational efforts. In 1834, the executive committee of the American Temperance Society acknowledged "that the influence of woman is essential to the triumph of every great and good cause; and should that influence which God has graciously given her, be . . . exerted in favor of the Temperance reformation, its triumphs would be certain and complete."[12] But women could not serve as officers of associations, or even official delegates to conventions, until they formed their own organizations in the 1840s.

Part of the explanation for women's exclusion was an effort to reinforce and revise gendered definitions of appropriate masculine and feminine roles in the Jacksonian era. From Barbara Welter's 1966 article on "The Cult of True Womanhood" to the studies in the 1990s, historians of women took seriously antebellum language of "separate spheres" for men and women. But historians no longer believe in the idea that men and women acted within physically separate spheres.[13] We have too many examples of women running taverns, taking in boarders, running businesses, and attending conventions and political rallies to believe that women stayed at home cleaning the house while men engaged in political and economic activity. In the late 1820s the first few farm girls began working as spinners in the cotton factories of Lowell. By the 1850s, one-quarter of all manufacturing jobs were filled by women, making them a crucial part of the public economic sphere.[14] However, while historians such as Linda K. Kerber have dismantled the idea of actual separate spheres, they continue to use the term to describe the beliefs that antebellum men and women had about gender and gender roles.[15]

Middle-class men and women believed that they each had separate and special values and traits. As Bruce Dorsey explains in *Re-*

forming Men and Women: Gender in the Antebellum City, those traits were under severe strain as the market revolution undermined male independence, turning artisans into wage workers and threatening men's ability to hold up their half of the marital agreement in which they provided economic support in exchange for women's obedience.[16] The temperance movement provided a new vision of masculinity, separating it from both the hard-drinking bar culture and male financial independence. It suggested that proper men not only had discipline, gentility, and the ability to work hard (even as dependent employees) but also the ability to be gentle, caring spouses. This new gendered identity was also a class identity that helped middle-class men differentiate themselves from a rapidly growing urban working class. In the North, it was not specifically a racial identity. While black men were not welcome in all temperance groups, wealthier ones did participate, articulating their own sense of middle-class masculinity. Many black people saw temperance as part of a strategy of "racial uplift" that would make them more economically successful and more worthy of white fellowship at the same time.[17] In the South, temperance reform was never as widespread as in the North. Where it did exist, it functioned as part of a broader effort to maintain white male control over dependents, including women and slaves.[18] While race was predominant in the South, class and gender were the crucial divisions in the North. This meant that working-class men (and eventually women) would have to form their own temperance organizations, thus further spreading and deepening the Age of Association.

In 1840, six artisans in Baltimore founded the Washingtonian Temperance Society for working-class men. The middle-class American Temperance Society focused on keeping middle-class men from falling into drunkenness and offered a condescending helping hand to the already fallen working class. In contrast, the Washingtonians focused on helping the working class help themselves. Far more sympathetic to the economic changes that might force a skilled artisan into unskilled, low-paid wage labor, the Washingtonians did not treat the drunkard as an evil man. Rather, they saw drinkers as victims who needed assistance to pull themselves up. At the same time, a Catholic temperance movement emerged among Irish immigrants, who had resented the Protestant middle-class reformers' anti-Catholic attitudes. These new organizations dramatically expanded the temperance movement, but they created difficult conflicts over goals and methods.

The term *temperance* had originally evolved from the middle-class goal of getting people to temper or reduce their drinking. Yet the middle class rapidly moved away from the idea of temperance to the goal of teetotalism, or abstention. Teetotalers wanted people to completely abstain from alcohol, seeing it as a black-and-white moral choice that divided the successful from the fallen. This change resulted in a parallel change in methods, from a movement primarily interested in influencing hearts and minds to one that saw the outlawing of alcohol sales as more immediately effective. By 1838, these "prohibition" advocates had already gotten politicians in Massachusetts, Connecticut, and Tennessee to restrict alcohol sales, and in 1851 they would celebrate as Maine became the first state to ban the sale of alcohol altogether.[19] Over time, debates over prohibition would be reflected in the platforms of the political parties of the Jacksonian era, with middle-class reformers voting for the Whig Party and Catholic Irish and many German immigrants voting for the Democrats. The white, working-class Washingtonians were often caught between parties, although they leaned toward the Democratic Party.

That so many men could vote on temperance issues was a result of changes in voting laws that preceded the antebellum period. Connecticut, Massachusetts, and New York dropped property requirements for voters in 1817-22, while Indiana, Illinois, Alabama, Missouri, and Maine became states with wide voting rights from the start.[20] This helped to fuel dramatic increases in political participation. It also made the creation of political organizations crucial for any population wanting to impose its vision on society, including temperance reformers. Yet as voting rights became disconnected from property ownership, gender became an increasingly important justification for the exclusion of women from the franchise.[21] Voting was increasingly defined as a male prerogative. However, the roles and rights of one gender can rarely change without provoking changes for the other gender. As men expanded their activity into the political realm, women claimed an increasingly large moral role in American society, serving in ever more visible roles in the public sphere.[22]

As the American Temperance Society had recognized in their 1834 resolution, women played a crucial role in the temperance movement. In addition to being a moral voice for temperance with husbands, brothers, and children, women were major fund-raisers and background organizers. The preachers of the Second Great Awakening had reinforced the idea that women had a particular moral responsibility in society, especially as husbands and sons faced the corrupting influences and moral compromises inherent in economic competition and political participation. Women were increasingly public in their support for temperance. They organized their own temperance societies where they could serve as officers and control the agenda. In upstate New York in 1849, Amelia Bloomer would become the first female editor of a temperance newspaper. She strongly encouraged women to become involved in temperance, particularly because women were seen as its most pitiful victims, beaten by drunken men or slowly starving as men drank away the family income. Bloomer recognized that women's temperance activism could be considered political and thus beyond woman's "proper sphere." In the first issue of her newspaper, she suggested that all temperance work "be conducted in a manner becoming the retiring modesty of our sex—without noise or parade, and in accordance with the strictest rules of propriety."[23] Yet Bloomer was also a signer of the Declaration of Rights and Sentiments in 1848 and called for women's right to vote, seeing a direct connection between her temperance work and women's need for more political influence. This conflict between two visions of a woman's appropriate role, whether moral and modest or moral and politically enfranchised, grew out of changing definitions of masculinity and femininity, shifting economic roles, and an expansion in the definition of human rights, which was particularly clear in the antislavery movement.

In *Creating the Culture of Reform in Antebellum America,* T. Gregory Garvey focuses on antislavery, women's rights, and a religious controversy, deliberately leaving out temperance. He argues that the temperance reformers were remarkably conservative in comparison to other reformers, a position also taken by earlier historians Ronald Walters and, less strongly, Steven Mintz.[24] While temperance reformers were quick to use the new communication and transportation technologies of the Jacksonian period to increase their fortunes and spread their message, they wanted to temper the massive changes inaugurated by the market revolution with a focus on conservative moral values. By comparison, antislavery activists were radicals. In fighting slavery, they were taking on one of the fundamental cornerstones of American economic and political development. As historians Michael Vorenberg and James M. McPherson have shown, the antislavery movement would contribute to the start of the Civil War, the end of slavery, and the beginning of a long civil rights movement for African American political and social equality.[25] Abolitionists also helped unsettle and then shatter the Jacksonian political parties, facilitated the creation of the modern Republican Party, and launched the women's rights movement. They were major contributors to the development of the Age of Association, creating not only national, state, county, and town antislavery societies but also two political parties and multiple organizations focused on the care of escaped and freed slaves.

Such a radical movement had conservative beginnings. In 1775, a group of white male legal and political elites in Philadelphia created the first and largest antislavery society, the Pennsylvania Abolition Society. This organization worked primarily to change the laws permitting slavery and was energized by the language and optimism spawned by the American Revolution. Their approach was challenged in 1816 when a group of prominent, primarily southern, white men founded the American Colonization Society

(ACS) to assist slave owners in shipping freed slaves back to Africa. They too hoped to gradually end slavery, but they rejected an interracial vision of America. They thought colonization was the only way to avoid the racial antagonism, retribution, or violence that many pessimistic or prejudiced Americans feared would result if large numbers of formerly enslaved black people remained in the country. By the early 1830s, free black resistance to the ideas of the ACS, more radical writings by British antislavery activists, and the ideas of the Second Great Awakening convinced a few men and women that a third strategy was necessary.[26]

In Philadelphia in 1833 an interracial group of middle-class men formed the American Anti-Slavery Society (AAS). This national society dedicated itself to the immediate end of slavery and was opposed to colonization. Black and white male activists joined William Lloyd Garrison, the editor of the antislavery newspaper the *Liberator,* to write a Declaration of Principles that declared slavery to be a sin and called on men and women to work toward its immediate eradication. The antislavery movement grew rapidly from 1833 to 1837, with dozens and then hundreds of antislavery societies developing across the North. Until the 1990s, Garrison was almost always credited as the radical force behind the AAS and the growth of abolition, and studies of him abound, including Henry Mayer's *All on Fire.*[27] However, historians have recognized that Garrison was deeply influenced by black male, white female, and black female activists. One of the first historians to stress the history of abolition prior to Garrison was Richard S. Newman, in *The Transformation of American Abolitionism.* Timothy Patrick McCarthy and John Stauffer's *Prophets of Protest: Reconsidering the History of American Abolitionism* is the latest work on black abolitionists, while Julie Roy Jeffrey's *The Great Silent Army of Abolitionism: Ordinary Women in the Antislavery Movement* and Beth A. Salerno's *Sister Societies: Women's Antislavery Organizations in Antebellum America* focus specifically on women's participation. John Stauffer's *The Black Hearts of Men* explores antislavery activists that we can now see were far more radical than Garrison.[28]

As with temperance, antislavery activists first focused on chang-ing hearts and minds—and behavior. Recognizing that slavery af-fected all Americans, not just those who held slaves, antislavery organizers called for abstention from slave products, including cotton and sugar. This precursor to modern activist boycotts was hampered by limited availability and poor quality. Lucretia Mott's granddaughter wrote that free-sugar candies were "an abomina-tion," while Boston activist Deborah Weston noted that her free-labor principles prohibited her from buying a new cotton gown, so she attempted to trade with others to update her wardrobe.[29] Yet boycotts were easier than the interracial socializing that many activists thought was a necessary corollary to their antislavery efforts. Antislavery activists Sarah and Angelina Grimké wrote that when they arrived late at an antislavery convention, multiple people got up to give them a seat. However, no one even spoke to the African American woman who had arrived with them, who stood for the entire event.[30] Antislavery activism did not necessar-ily mean activism for equal rights.

Antislavery efforts were met with severe resistance in both the South and the North. In the South, Nat Turner's violent and un-successful slave rebellion in 1831 brought new and harsher laws limiting slaves and a new proslavery attitude that silenced most antislavery efforts. Proslavery (or anti-antislavery) violence spread across the North with riots in Utica, New York; Boston, Massa-chusetts; Providence, Rhode Island; Concord, New Hampshire; Philadelphia, Pennsylvania; and many other cities. In 1838, in Philadelphia, rioters burned down the antislavery lecture hall as well as buildings that housed black orphanages and businesses.[31] This wave of violence, combined with the Panic of 1837, slowed the organization of new societies, but men and women continued to petition Congress in huge numbers. The House of Represen-tatives was so overwhelmed with the sheer volume of petitions and the resulting endless debates over slavery that they finally banned receipt and reading of all antislavery petitions. This "gag rule" raised crucial issues about the right to petition and to be heard by one's political representatives, drawing many otherwise unsympathetic people to the antislavery cause. It was of particular importance to women, who had no other recognized method for influencing the political system. The power of women's petitions is best examined in Susan Zaeske's *Signatures of Citizenship: Petitioning, Antislavery, and Women's Political Identity.*[32]

By 1840 the antislavery movement was at a crossroads. Two critical events happened that year, which divided the movement and created many new organizations. First, in London, female delegates from American antislavery societies were denied entrance into a World Anti-Slavery Convention. The organizers claimed that only men could serve as public representatives of antislavery organizations. This break had been brewing for at least three years in America as women and men kept up a very public debate on women's appropriate role in the antislavery movement. Two South Carolina natives, Angelina and Sarah Grimké, became prominent antislavery speakers, and in 1837 they were chastised by Congregational ministers for addressing large crowds of men and women, which the ministers felt was beyond woman's appropriate sphere. The Grimkés responded by writing and publishing books defending a woman's right to act publically, even politically, in a moral cause.[33] The American Anti-Slavery Society and various state societies split into competing associations, supporters of women's right to participate in one organization and critics in the other. Two women who were deeply offended by the exclusion in London were Lucretia Mott and Elizabeth Cady Stanton. Eight years later they would meet again in Seneca Falls to demand not only the right to speak at conventions but also the right to vote in national elections.[34]

In 1840 the other critical event was the foundation of the first antislavery political party. While abolitionists were debating the role of women, they were also divided over the question of methods. Some abolitionists, including the prominent William Lloyd Garrison, believed that both political institutions and churches were corrupted by their compromises with slavery and that true antislavery activists could participate in neither. This deeply offended ministers and many religious people, some of whom left the movement to pursue other reforms, particularly missionary work. Other abolitionists felt strongly that political involvement was the most effective and direct way to change the political rules that permitted slavery to continue. Moving from petitioning to voting seemed a clear and logical progression, and political abolitionists hoped to win support from the Whig Party. But when Henry Clay, a prominent senator vying for the Whig nomination for president, made a Senate speech in 1839 declaring that neither the Democratic Party nor the Whig Party could be "justly accused of any Abolition tendency or purpose," some abolitionists felt the need for another option.[35] At a snowbound convention in Albany, New York, in January 1840, abolitionists nominated independent candidates for president and vice president under the banner of the Liberty Party. The party had a terrible first showing as they struggled to get organized. Many abolitionists were not willing to risk a vote that could profitably be cast against Jackson's heir, Martin Van Buren. Liberty Party support for an end to discrimination against northern blacks did not help their cause with most voters either.[36] For this reason, historians have generally not taken the party as seriously as later parties, although a new book by Reinhard O. Johnson, *The Liberty Party, 1840–1848: Antislavery Third-Party Politics in the United States,* challenges that attitude.[37]

Eventually politicians including Senator Salmon P. Chase would draw Liberty voters into a broader coalition with weaker antislavery principles. This Free Soil Party would emerge in part from the Mexican-American War of 1846–48 and America's acquisition of huge western territories. It focused less on the elimination of slavery and more on stopping the extension of slavery into new areas. The free-soil message would also resonate with a Jacksonian vision of working-class masculinity that stressed the power of free labor to shape strong, independent, Republican men. Thus American workers felt a strong need to keep the new American territories free from demoralizing economic competition with slave labor. The motto "Free Soil, Free Labor, Free Men" would carry this 1848 party through two elections (and give historian Eric Foner the title of his book *Free Soil, Free Labor, Free Men: The Ideology of the Republican Party before the Civil War*).[38] The Free Soil

Party would be absorbed into the political coalition that became the Republican Party in 1854. Republicans offered varied levels of support for antislavery efforts until near the close of the Civil War, although southerners saw the election of Abraham Lincoln in 1861 as a threat to their political power and as a real barrier against further expansion of slavery. Their fears led to secession, the attack on Fort Sumter, and the beginning of the Civil War.

The historiography of antislavery is a model of how each generation of historians can find new meaning and importance in a particular topic. After the Civil War, most writers about abolition had been abolitionists. In books such as Parker Pillsbury's *Acts of the Anti-Slavery Apostles* or Samuel J. May's *Some Recollections of Our Antislavery Conflict,* the authors celebrated the abolitionists as visionaries who had seen how slavery would lead to bloody conflict and who had helped to bring America to a fuller realization of its destiny as a place of liberty and justice. As evidence, they noted that male and female abolitionists had pushed Lincoln to enact some kind of emancipation proclamation and then engaged in the largest petition campaign in history to get Congress to enact the Thirteenth Amendment, which made slavery unconstitutional.[39] Yet in the 1930s and 1940s, some historians were vilifying abolitionists as fanatics who had helped to cause one of the most divisive and bloody wars in American history. This debate continued for many years, transforming over time into a debate on the success or failure of antislavery activists, summed up best in Merton L. Dillon's article "The Failure of the American Abolitionists."[40] The civil rights movement reinvigorated interest in the antislavery movement, with historians paying sympathetic attention to its strategies and goals. The women's movement of the 1970s brought new attention to women's roles in the antislavery effort and the connection between antislavery and women's rights through works by Keith E. Melder, Ellen Carol DuBois, and Blanche Glassman Hersh.[41] A wave of interest in American political development shaped the 1980s and 1990s, drawing attention to antislavery activists' pioneering roles in creating third parties and infusing moral imperatives into politics, particularly Alan M. Kraut's *Crusaders and Compromisers* and Lori D.

Ginzberg's *Women and the Work of Benevolence.*[42] Now historians
have further deepened the field by studying antislavery families
(Chris Dixon, *Perfecting the Family*) and by examining the gendered
beliefs that shaped antislavery policies among male and female activists within the Republican Party (Michael D. Pierson, *Free Hearts
and Free Homes*).[43] In many ways, the historiography of antislavery,
like that of temperance and women's rights, has moved far beyond
the Age of Association to specifically study the long chronological
sweep and international influences of these three movements.[44] But
if we focus on the antebellum period, we can identify two central
issues—the changing definition of gender roles and the changing
boundaries of politics—which will provide rich ground for further
study. Both of these are already central to historians' understanding
of the women's rights movement.

As noted earlier, women's participation in both the temperance
movement and the antislavery movement was constrained by social ideas about appropriate roles for men and women. No women
were officially invited as delegates to the 1833 meeting that founded
the American Anti-Slavery Society and none were asked to sign the
official Declaration of Principles. As Lucretia Mott would reminisce
thirty years later, "I do not think it occurred to any one of us at
that time that there would be a propriety in [women] signing the
[Declaration of Principles]."[45] Even as late as 1853, female delegates
were barred from a World Temperance Convention. The widespread number of associations in the antebellum period resulted
partly from the many needs of the period but also because each
gender—and often each class and race as well—formed separate
organizations.

Yet the market revolution and the Second Great Awakening
were rapidly changing the boundaries of both masculinity and
femininity. Many middle-class women moved from production to
consumption as they were able to now shop for the soap, candles,
food, and clothing they used to have to make. This gave them time
to invest in the church-sanctioned female activity of caring for the
less fortunate through participation in moral reform, temperance,
antislavery, Sunday school societies, or dozens of other associa-

tions.[46] Antislavery women found that speaking for the "dumb and the oppressed" and challenging society's moral lapses were deeply political activities, as slavery was supported by the Constitution and people eventually came to believe that it could only be eradicated by political means. Women began to petition Congress and support their husbands, brothers, and sons in campaigns for antislavery political candidates. A few edited newspapers for antislavery political parties. These activities created a new understanding of woman's appropriate role, linking her benevolent work and its political implications directly to the center of her domestic role. As the women of the Massachusetts Female Emancipation Society wrote, "If woman has nothing to do with politics then has she nothing to do with the rising generation; then has she no duty to her husband,—none to her neighbor,—in fine none to the world; then indeed must she needs *go out of the world* to seek her duties."[47] Even in the home, women could turn a feminine tea party into a political event by putting free-labor sugar in a sugar bowl adorned with an image of a slave woman in chains. The motto "Am I Not a Woman and a Sister?" printed in bold letters would make her antislavery beliefs clear to every guest, even though she had neither left the domestic sphere nor engaged in any voting-related activity.

Thus some middle-class, white, antislavery women found themselves stretching the boundaries of the domestic sphere to include political activity and expanding their expected role to include agitation on behalf of the poor and oppressed. Some temperance women soon followed as that movement turned to the political system to outlaw the sale of alcohol. It was a small intellectual step for women to demand the right to vote in order to protect their husbands, homes, and children from the ravages of alcohol or the national sin of slavery. Yet this was a huge challenge to traditional understandings of a woman's role. Most Americans assumed that women had to keep their distance from politics in order to serve as a moral, virtuous force countering the corrupting forces of political compromise and economic competition to which men were increasingly exposed every day. Thus many women would reject the call for women's rights and the right to vote. They claimed it distracted from their reform efforts and undermined the female virtue that pushed women to reform in the first place. Elizabeth Cady Stanton would serve as president of the New York Women's State Temperance Organization for only one year before more conservative women ousted her because they disagreed with her call for female suffrage.[48] But whether or not women agreed on suffrage, they all implicitly agreed that women had a critical and necessary role in the public sphere, influencing public policy toward greater morality.

The women's rights movement of the Jacksonian period was predominantly a white, middle-class movement. Working-class women would organize for more immediate needs, including shorter days and higher pay at the Lowell factories.[49] Black women participated in both the temperance and antislavery movements, though they faced discrimination in both. Often they would found their own societies to give themselves more power and control and to link their work to the uplift of black communities.[50] Since black men could not vote in most states, black women found it problematic to argue for their own enfranchisement. In addition, racism within the women's suffrage movement often excluded black women from those organizations.[51] These divisions would limit the women's rights movement into the twentieth century but were reflections of the racial and economic realities of the Jacksonian period. The Seneca Falls Declaration of Rights and Sentiments was signed primarily by white, middle-class women. It aimed to expand opportunities for and reduce limitations on these women. This group would have been most likely to benefit from the educational and employment opportunities they demanded, including medical, law, and ministerial training, as well as the right to divorce and to have custody of children. Their activism, combined with that of concerned fathers, resulted in married women's property laws that protected a woman's inherited and earned property from ne'er-do-well husbands. But black and working-class women participated in the expansion of the public sphere, giving public lectures, engaging in new forms of work, and appearing before state legislatures on behalf of antidiscrimination and working-woman legislation. A few

were present at Seneca Falls. In this way, the women's rights movement affected almost every female constituency in antebellum
America.[52]

Historians of the Jacksonian period have been slow to fully integrate the study of women and reform into the broader historiography. The most widely praised synthesis of Jacksonian scholarship, *Liberty and Power,* by Harry L. Watson, is subtitled *The Politics
of Jacksonian America.* This is no accident, as the study of politics,
whether inside the voting booths or outside in street demonstra-
tions, still dominates scholarship of the antebellum period. Charles
Sellers succeeded in integrating the study of economic and political
change in *The Market Revolution,* but Watson notes that historians'
efforts to integrate religion and reform into that synthesis have not
been nearly as successful.[53] Historians have made progress in recognizing the role played by women. Writing about antebellum history prior to the 1990s, Watson noted, "No matter how much they
may have disagreed about other matters, one thing most Jacksonian historians have taken for granted has been that politics mostly
concerned men. The voters and officeholders were all male, and
traditionally so were most of the historians. In their view, American women were mostly willing nonparticipants in the Jacksonian
political stag party." Times have changed. In 2006, Watson stressed
that Jacksonian historians "can never again assume that women
were irrelevant to nineteenth-century public life."[54]

Yet public life and politics are not the same thing. Watson only
cites books that connect women directly to the political parties
(such as Elizabeth R. Varon's *We Mean to Be Counted*) rather than to
a changing definition of politics, where setting the agenda, creating the language, and influencing the candidates might prove more
important than casting a vote.[55] The temperance, antislavery, and
women's rights movements had crucial implications for the Jacksonian era in the creation of new political constituencies, the development of new political techniques and parties, a politicization of
the domestic sphere, and an infusion of female language and issues
into the political debates of the day. But if we look beyond politics,
we see that these movements may have been equally important for

other reasons. All three challenged and redefined antebellum gender roles. Temperance and antislavery challenged people to avoid immoral consumption, whether of slave-made products or enslaving alcohol, tying these movements directly to changing consumption patterns generated by the market revolution. All three drew on the transportation revolutions of the period and contributed to the communication revolution by rapidly expanding the number of newspapers, pamphlets, tracts, and books available to a broad reading public. Jacksonian historians still have a challenge before them to fully integrate these movements into histories of the antebellum era. The rewards of a new synthesis will be a more inclusive history that helps us to better understand this period often named after a president but defined by the power, number, reach, and impact of its associations.

NOTES

1. Elizabeth Cady Stanton, Susan B. Anthony, and Matilda Joslyn Gage, *History of Woman Suffrage,* vol. 1 (1881; New York: Arno Press, 1969), 70. Italics added for emphasis.

2. Arch Merrill, as quoted in Judith Wellman, *The Road to Seneca Falls: Elizabeth Cady Stanton and the First Woman's Rights Convention* (Urbana: Univ. of Illinois Press, 2004), 11; Ellen Carol DuBois, *Feminism and Suffrage: The Emergence of an Independent Women's Movement in America, 1848-1869* (Ithaca, N.Y.: Cornell Univ. Press, 1978); Jean Baker, *Votes for Women: The Struggle for Suffrage Revisited* (New York: Oxford Univ. Press, 2002).

3. Daniel Walker Howe, *What Hath God Wrought: The Transformation of America, 1815-1848* (New York: Oxford Univ. Press, 2007), 4-5.

4. Alexis de Tocqueville, *Democracy in America,* trans. Harvey C. Mansfield and Delba Winthrop (Chicago: Univ. of Chicago Press, 2000), 489.

5. Sally Gregory McMillen, *Seneca Falls and the Origins of the Women's Rights Movement* (New York: Oxford Univ. Press, 2008), 84-89.

6. Daniel Feller, *The Jacksonian Promise: America, 1815-1840* (Baltimore: Johns Hopkins Univ. Press, 1995).

7. Holly Berkley Fletcher, *Gender and the American Temperance Movement of the Nineteenth Century* (New York: Routledge, 2008), 8.

8. Bruce Dorsey, *Reforming Men and Women: Gender in the Antebellum City* (Ithaca, N.Y.: Cornell Univ. Press, 2002), 91.

9. "The Rewards of Drunkenness," tract no. 159, *The Temperance Volume,* 4, as quoted in Fletcher, *Gender and the American Temperance Movement,* 9.

10. Whitney R. Cross, *The Burned-over District: The Social and Intellectual History of Enthusiastic Religion in Western New York, 1800-1850* (Ithaca, N.Y.: Cornell Univ. Press, 1950); James Brewer Stewart, *Holy Warriors: The Abolitionists and American Slavery,* rev. ed. (New York: Hill and Wang, 1996), 36; Steven Mintz, *Moralists and Modernizers: America's Pre-Civil War Reformers* (Baltimore: Johns Hopkins Univ. Press, 1995); Robert H. Abzug, *Cosmos Crumbling: American Reform and the Religious Imagination* (New York: Oxford Univ. Press, 1994), 58-59.

11. Lyman Beecher, *Six Sermons on the Nature, Occasions, Signs, Evils, and Remedy of Intemperance* (New York: American Tract Society, 1827).

12. Fletcher, *Gender and the American Temperance Movement,* 16; American Temperance Union, *Permanent Temperance Documents of the American Temperance Society* (New York: American Temperance Union, 1843), 3.

13. Barbara Welter, "The Cult of True Womanhood: 1820-1860," *American Quarterly* 18, no. 2 (1966): pt. 1.

14. McMillen, *Seneca Falls and the Origins of the Women's Rights Movement,* 30.

15. Linda K. Kerber, "Separate Spheres, Female Worlds, Woman's Place: The Rhetoric of Women's History," *Journal of American History* 75, no. 1 (1988): 9-39; Kim Warren, "Separate Spheres: Analytical Persistence in United States Women's History," *History Compass* 5, no. 1 (2007): 262-77.

16. Dorsey, *Reforming Men and Women,* esp. chaps. 1 and 4.

17. Fletcher, *Gender and the American Temperance Movement,* 47-48.

18. There is very little written on temperance in the South. See Douglas Carlson, "'Drinks He to His Own Undoing': Temperance Ideology in the Deep South," *Journal of the Early Republic* 18 (1998): 659-91. For a broader comparison of the movement in the North and South, see John W. Quist, *Restless Visionaries: The Social Roots of Antebellum Reform in Alabama and Michigan* (Baton Rouge: Louisiana State Univ. Press, 1998).

19. Fletcher, *Gender and the American Temperance Movement,* 22.

20. Feller, *Jacksonian Promise,* 67.

21. McMillen, *Seneca Falls and the Origins of the Women's Rights Movement,* 29-30.

22. T. Gregory Garvey, *Creating the Culture of Reform in Antebellum America* (Athens: Univ. of Georgia Press, 2006), 29.

23. Amelia Bloomer, "Woman's Work in the Temperance Cause," *Lily* 1/4 (1849): 21, as quoted in Scott C. Martin, *Devil of the Domestic Sphere: Temperance, Gender, and Middle-Class Ideology, 1800-1860* (Dekalb: Northern Illinois Univ. Press, 2008), 143.

24. Garvey, *Creating the Culture of Reform in Antebellum America,* 3-4; Mintz, *Moralists and Modernizers,* 72-73; Ronald G. Walters, *American Reformers, 1815-1860* (New York: Hill and Wang, 1978), 141.

25. Michael Vorenberg, *Final Freedom: The Civil War, the Abolition of Slavery, and the Thirteenth Amendment* (New York: Cambridge Univ. Press, 2001); James M. McPherson, *The Abolitionist Legacy: From Reconstruction to the NAACP* (Princeton, N.J.: Princeton Univ. Press, 1975).

26. Eric Burin, *Slavery and the Peculiar Solution: A History of the American Colonization Society* (Gainesville: Univ. Press of Florida, 2005).

27. Henry Mayer, *All on Fire: William Lloyd Garrison and the Abolition of Slavery* (New York: St. Martin's Press, 1998).

28. Richard S. Newman, *The Transformation of American Abolitionism: Fighting Slavery in the Early Republic* (Chapel Hill: Univ. of North Carolina Press, 2002); Timothy Patrick McCarthy and John Stauffer, *Prophets of Protest: Reconsidering the History of American Abolitionism* (New York: New Press, distributed by W. W. Norton, 2006); Julie Roy Jeffrey, *The Great Silent Army of Abolitionism: Ordinary Women in the Antislavery Movement* (Chapel Hill: Univ. of North Carolina Press, 1998); Beth A. Salerno, *Sister Societies: Women's Antislavery Organizations in Antebellum America* (DeKalb: Northern Illinois Univ. Press, 2005); John Stauffer, *The Black Hearts of Men: Radical Abolitionists and the Transformation of Race* (Cambridge, Mass.: Harvard Univ. Press, 2002).

29. Anna Davis Hallowell, ed., *James and Lucretia Mott: Life and Letters* (Boston: Houghton, Mifflin and Co., 1884), 88; ALS from Deborah Weston to Aunt Mary, Boston, June 15, 1837, Ms.A.9.2.9.42, Boston Public Library.

30. Laura H. Lovell, *Report of a Delegate to the Anti-Slavery Convention of American Women. Held in Philadelphia, May, 1838* (Boston: J. Knapp, 1838), 14.

31. John R. McKivigan and Stanley Harrold, *Antislavery Violence: Sectional, Racial, and Cultural Conflict in Antebellum America* (Knoxville: Univ. of Tennessee Press, 1999); Leonard L. Richards, *Gentlemen of Property and Standing: Anti-Abolition Mobs in Jacksonian America* (New York: Oxford Univ. Press, 1970).

32. Susan Zaeske, *Signatures of Citizenship: Petitioning, Antislavery, and Women's Political Identity* (Chapel Hill: Univ. of North Carolina Press, 2003).

33. "Pastoral Letter," *Genius of Universal Emancipation,* Aug. 11, 1837; Angelina E. Grimké, *Letters to Catherine E. Beecher, in Reply to an Essay on Slavery and Abolitionism, Addressed to A. E. Grimké, Revised by the Author* (Boston: Isaac Knapp, 1838); Sarah M. Grimké, *Letters on the Equality of the Sexes and the Condition of Women, Addressed to Mary S. Parker, President of the Boston Female Anti-Slavery Society* (Boston: Isaac Knapp, 1838).

34. Kathryn Kish Sklar, "Women Who Speak for an Entire Nation," in *The Abolitionist Sisterhood: Women's Political Culture in Antebellum America,* ed. Jean Fagan Yellin and John C. Van Horne (Ithaca, N.Y.: Cornell Univ. Press, 1994): 301-33.

35. As quoted in Richard H. Sewell, *Ballots for Freedom: Antislavery Politics in the United States, 1837-1860* (New York: W. W. Norton and Company, 1976), 49.

36. Ibid., 69-72, 76, 97-98.

37. Reinhard O. Johnson, *The Liberty Party, 1840-1848: Antislavery Third-Party Politics in the United States* (Baton Rouge: Louisiana State Univ. Press, 2009).

38. Eric Foner, *Free Soil, Free Labor, Free Men: The Ideology of the Republican Party before the Civil War* (New York: Oxford Univ. Press, 1970).

39. Parker Pillsbury, *Acts of the Anti-Slavery Apostles* (Concord, N.H.: Clague, Wegman, Schlict, 1883); Samuel J. May, *Some Recollections of Our Antislavery Conflict* (Boston: Fields, Osgood, and Co., 1869).

40. Merton L. Dillon, "The Failure of the American Abolitionists," *Journal of Southern History* 25, no. 2 (1959): 159-77; Merton L. Dillon, "The Abolitionists: A Decade of Historiography, 1959-1969," *Journal of Southern History* 35, no. 4 (1969): 500-522.

41. Keith E. Melder, *Beginnings of Sisterhood: The American Woman's Rights Movement, 1800-1850* (New York: Schocken Books, 1977); Ellen Carol DuBois, "Women's Rights and Abolition: The Nature of the Connection," and Blanche Glassman Hersh, "'Am I Not a Woman and a Sister?': Abolitionist Beginnings of Nineteenth-Century Feminism," both in Lewis Perry and Michael Fellman, eds., *Antislavery Reconsidered: New Perspectives on the Abolitionists,* (Baton Rouge: Louisiana State Univ. Press, 1979), 238-51 and 252-83, respectively.

42. Alan M. Kraut, *Crusaders and Compromisers: Essays on the Relationship of the Antislavery Struggle to the Antebellum Party System* (Westport, Conn.: Greenwood Press, 1983); Lori D. Ginzberg, *Women and the Work of Benevolence: Morality, Politics, and Class in the Nineteenth-Century United States* (New Haven, Conn.: Yale Univ. Press, 1990).

43. Chris Dixon, *Perfecting the Family: Antislavery Marriages in Nineteenth-Century America* (Amherst: Univ. of Massachusetts Press, 1997); Michael D. Pierson, *Free Hearts and Free Homes: Gender and American Antislavery Politics* (Chapel Hill: Univ. of North Carolina Press, 2003).

44. See, for example, Kathryn Kish Sklar and James Brewer Stewart, *Women's Rights and Transatlantic Antislavery in the Era of Emancipation* (New Haven, Conn.: Yale Univ. Press, 2007).

45. American Anti-Slavery Society, *Proceedings of the American Anti-Slavery Society at Its Third Decade, Held in the City of Philadelphia, Dec. 3d and 4th, 1863* (New York: American Anti-Slavery Society, 1864), 41-43.

46. Anne M. Boylan, *The Origins of Women's Activism: New York and Boston, 1797-1840* (Chapel Hill: Univ. of North Carolina Press, 2002).

47. Massachusetts Female Emancipation Society, *First Annual Report of the Massachusetts Female Emancipation Society* (Boston: James Loring, 1841), 8.

48. Fletcher, *Gender and the American Temperance Movement,* 40-41.

49. Thomas Dublin, *Transforming Women's Work: New England Lives in the Industrial Revolution* (Ithaca, N.Y.: Cornell Univ. Press, 1994).

50. Shirley J. Yee, *Black Women Abolitionists: A Study in Activism, 1828-1860* (Knoxville: Univ. of Tennessee Press, 1992).

51. Rosalyn Terborg-Penn, *African American Women in the Struggle for the Vote, 1850-1920* (Bloomington: Indiana Univ. Press, 1998).

52. On black women, see the articles by Emma Lapsansky, Julie Winch, and Anne Boylan in Jean Fagan Yellin and John C. Van Horne, eds., *The Abolitionist Sisterhood: Women's Political Culture in Antebellum America* (Ithaca, N.Y.: Cornell Univ. Press, 1994).

53. Harry L. Watson, *Liberty and Power: The Politics of Jacksonian America* (New York: Hill and Wang, 2006), 257; Melvyn Stokes and Stephen Conway, *The Market Revolution in America: Social, Political, and Religious Expressions, 1800-1880* (Charlottesville: Univ. Press of Virginia, 1996).

54. Watson, *Liberty and Power,* 270-71.

55. Elizabeth R. Varon, *We Mean to Be Counted: White Women and Politics in Antebellum Virginia* (Chapel Hill: Univ. of North Carolina Press, 1998).

CHAPTER SEVEN

"The Few at the Expense of the Many"

The Historiography of Jacksonian Economics

RYAN RUCKEL

"If we can not at once . . . make our Government what it ought to be, we can at least take a stand against all new grants of monopolies and exclusive privileges, against any prostitution of our Government to the advancement of the few at the expense of the many," declared Andrew Jackson in his 1832 veto message. Jackson's veto spelled the beginning of the end for the Second Bank of the United States (BUS).[1] Indeed, Jackson waged a political war against the BUS, a struggle every bit as difficult as his wars against the British and the Indians, yet in his mind even more vital to the nation's future. Twenty-first-century Americans, most of whom may never have heard of Jackson's Bank War, have grown accustomed to a large, powerful national government and an economy more prosperous and complex than any in the history of the world. Since the creation of the Federal Reserve System in 1913, Americans have tended to see federal involvement in the economy as necessary, or at least as a necessary evil, but Jackson would have seen it as a return of "the monster," the Second Bank of the United States.

Jackson's constituents came to hate the BUS because they thought of themselves as the political descendants of Thomas Jefferson. Jefferson's rival, Alexander Hamilton, had called for a central bank as part of his plan for a strong national government built upon a strong national economy, and good Jeffersonians feared any concentration of political and economic power as a deadly threat to liberty and the Republic. For their part, Hamiltonians such as Henry Clay believed they were reading the Constitution correctly when they sought to use the power of the national government to strengthen that same government and thus ensure its survival in a dangerous world, and they feared the "mob rule" that could put dictators in power. Clay's economic plan, known as the "American System," called for a high tariff to protect young American industries; for federal money to be spent on roads, bridges, and canals in order to facilitate commerce; and for a national bank to establish a national currency and stabilize the money supply. Jackson deeply mistrusted Clay, declaring that the BUS and other aspects of the American System had "arrayed section against section, interest against interest, and man against man, in a fearful commotion which threatens to shake the foundations of our Union."[2]

The BUS had emerged as a solution to the dual problem of fighting the War of 1812 without a central bank and of the chaotic banking situation that surfaced after the War of 1812. By the time the war ended in 1815, the number of small banks had expanded rapidly. Banks printed their own notes and were in a headlong rush to sell loans to the thousands of settlers moving west. Both bankers and settlers hoped to make money by speculating in land values, buying large tracts of cheap land and then selling the land later at a premium. The value of the nation's currency therefore fluctuated from place to place and from bank to bank, and the speculation in land encouraged an inflationary currency that badly needed stabilization. As a remedy, Congress chartered the BUS, a public-private institution that would provide a more uniform value for the notes in circulation.

Even so, the BUS operated as a profit-making corporation. The BUS engaged in its own land speculations, and it also acted as the sole repository for federal deposits, which included monies from land sales, customs duties, and even the postal service. The BUS soon became a clearinghouse for a rapidly expanding currency energized by rampant speculation. To meet its own financial obligations coming due in 1819, the bank, under the direction of its new president, Langdon Cheves, began calling in its loans and redeeming the notes it was holding from the state-chartered banks. The sudden, drastic contraction threw the state banks into insolvency and panic. In turn, the state banks had to call in their loans and notes, which led to sudden bankruptcies, significant unemployment, and startling depreciation of currency throughout most of the United States, with the frontier areas being hit the hardest and New England generally suffering less than the other sections.[3]

Ten years later, when Jackson became president of the United States, he made the BUS and other elements of the American System central issues in his first administration. For example, he considered his stand against the bank to be consistent with his stand against using federal money to build a road near Maysville, Kentucky, in 1830. The Maysville Road bill proposed using federal money to purchase stock in a company that would extend a road between Maysville and Lexington, Kentucky. Jackson vetoed the bill because he believed it unconstitutional and morally wrong for federal support to favor one state over another: "My feelings being now as it was on the Maysville Road bill, and the Bank veto; 'that it is a duty I owe to my country, my conscience and my god' to put down this mammoth of corruption and to separate it from being the agent of the Government as early as possible for the safety of its fiscal concerns." Jackson and his followers saw the issue as a moral menace that would destroy traditional liberties.[4]

Without question, Jackson's republican attitude toward the BUS has provided both his critics and his supporters, past as well as present, with a tidy, symbolic representation of the most essential elements of Jackson's character and political thought. Under the direction of Cheves and his successor, Nicholas Biddle, the BUS had become solvent, respected, and increasingly even more powerful. It had millions of dollars in capital to dispense through its branch banks, and it also served as the chief financial institution for the U.S. government. The BUS had also gained overwhelming influence over the nation's finances. When he first addressed Congress in 1829, Jackson attacked the bank's right to exist under the Constitution and remained dedicated to its dissolution thereafter. The BUS was due for recharter in 1836, but Jackson's opponents thought it would make an excellent campaign tool, useful for demonstrating Jackson's poorly controlled temper and the threat he posed to the financial security of the country.

Led by Henry Clay, friends of the bank pushed an early recharter bill through Congress in time for the 1832 election, goading Jackson into a veto. Jackson sought to destroy the bank on the grounds that a private institution should not be allowed to profit by managing public funds, that even when the bank's operators performed their duties with integrity and impartiality they directly benefitted from their connections to governmental power, and that one such corrupt relationship would spread corruption to the rest of the union. If government were to serve the interests of all equally, government could not favor a few with inside information, special connections, and ready access to public wealth. "The rich and powerful too often bend the acts of government to their selfish purposes," wrote Jackson, and in his mind the BUS represented an irresistible lure to the most corrupt of society's "best" citizens.[5]

From Jackson's point of view, a republic could not survive if its people did not respect the laws, which they would not do unless they believed that the laws applied equally to all. If citizens believed that playing by the rules would be rewarded with injustice and loss, then their virtuous adherence to law and their sacrifices for the good of the country were made a mockery, and eventually, he believed, the Republic would collapse under the burden of bearing up a government dependent on the goodness of a people who no longer behaved honorably toward each other. Inequality was a fact of life for Jackson. As he saw it, "Distinction in society will always exist under every just government. Equality of talents, of education, or of wealth can not be produced by human institutions."[6]

Jackson believed that those who had done well with what was given them owed a debt of virtuous behavior to the society that had made it possible for them to pursue their ambitions, and he believed that those who did not do so were violating a fundamental principle of the relationship between man and Providence. "In the full enjoyment of the gifts of Heaven and the fruits of superior industry, economy, and virtue, every man is equally entitled to protection by law," he wrote. "But when the laws undertake to add to these natural and just advantages artificial distinctions, to grant titles, gratuities, and exclusive privileges, to make the rich richer and the potent more powerful, the humble members of society—the farmers, mechanics, and laborers—who have neither the time nor the means of securing like favors to themselves, have a right to complain of the injustice of their Government." The public majority sympathized with Jackson's position and re-elected him in a landslide victory over Clay, his chief opponent in 1832. The victory gave Jackson his great redoubt against his critics' offensive, for he had appealed to the virtue of the American people. In his mind, they had not failed the test, and now he had an obligation before them and "under Heaven" to proceed against the incipient threat to that virtue, the BUS.[7]

Jackson often referred to the BUS as a "monster," a monster fed by the massive amounts of money deposited with it by the federal government. To "starve" the monster, Jackson ordered federal deposits relocated to state-chartered banks, usually to banks somehow favorable to the administration. Because Jackson played favorites with the federal deposits, the state banks who received them came to be known as "pet banks." In what might be considered a case of destroying the village in order to save it, Jackson had cut off at its base the entire American System of finance and banking and grafted it back to its original root stock, effectively returning it to the chaotic conditions that prevailed between 1815 and 1819. The move revealed some perplexing contradictions in Jackson's ideology. He had argued that all private and public monies ought to be kept separate in order to avoid corruption, yet he gave millions of federal dollars to unregulated, privately owned state banks friendly to his administration.

Jackson attacked the proliferation of paper money, saying that its unreliability and fluctuations in value swindled the common man out of the value of his own wages or property and could lead him to ruin with his creditors, yet by moving the deposits Jackson only encouraged the kind of speculation in paper notes that had led to the Panic of 1819. The monster was not yet dead, however, and Biddle struck back by restricting the bank's loans. So powerful was the bank that its reduction in credit threw the national economy into a contraction in 1833, which Biddle hoped would force a reconsideration of the bill for the bank's recharter. He reasoned that once people saw how much of their prosperity depended on having a strong BUS, they would clamor for its recharter. Instead, his gamble only convinced Jackson and the president's many supporters that they had correctly marked the bank as a bastion of aristocracy, corruption, and arrogance. The enormity of the struggle against the bank staggered the imagination of both friends and enemies of the BUS. As though he were assaulting an enemy position, Jackson had dug beneath what he saw as a fortress built of unearned wealth and unwarranted privilege, eliminating its source of strength, the federal deposits. By 1836 the bank had reverted to its original status as just another state-chartered bank, distinguished only by its massive, imposing porticoes overshadowing the colonial-era neighborhood surrounding Liberty Hall in Philadelphia, Pennsylvania.

Jackson drew the lesson carefully for Andrew Jackson Jr., his adopted son: "My conscience told me it was right to stop the career of this corrupting monster. I took the step fearlessly believing it a duty I owed to my god and my country. Providence smiles upon the act and all the virtuous of the land sustains it. . . . The history of my administration will be read with interest years after I am dead, and I trust will be the means of perpetuation of our happy Union and our liberties with it."[8]

Jackson was not wrong. Generations of historians have tried to understand Jackson, correct him, punish him, blame him, or apologize for him, goals for which the Bank War has often served as a symbolic representation of the Jacksonians' views on many other subjects. Just as they did in his day, commentators on Jackson still tend to be Democrat or Whig, "fer him or agin him," in their thinking. Not coincidentally, one of Jackson's earliest historians and critics, William Graham Sumner, wrote *A History of American Currency* and *Andrew Jackson as a Public Man: What He Was, What Chances He Had, and What He Did with Them.* Sumner, himself a hard-money, laissez-faire, free-trade, limited-government social Darwinist, should have found common ground with Jackson's views, but he saw Jackson's assault on the bank as an abuse of executive power that would eventually expand the influence of government. "Jacksonian democracy was approaching already the Napoleonic type of the democratic empire, in which 'the elect of the nation' is charged to protect the state against everybody, chiefly, however, against any constitutional organs."[9] Sumner often painted Jackson as an unschooled, undisciplined "Napoleon" whose cronies had pursued their own special advantages by making Jackson the tool with which they could attack the BUS, but he also shied away from blaming Jackson totally for the Panic of 1837. He pointed instead to world market changes, such as the fluctuating price of cotton, as contributing factors. Ralph C. H. Catterall and Reginald Charles McGrane then extended Sumner's analysis into full-blown indictments of Jackson and his policies. Catterall claimed in *The Second Bank of the United States* that the BUS had given America a sound currency, which Jackson had destroyed when he killed the bank. McGrane took Jackson to task in *The Panic of 1837: Some Financial Problems of the Jacksonian Era,* blaming him fully for the panic and holding the general's ignorance up for ridicule. Between them, these early professional historians set the tone and terms of the debate for several generations of Jacksonian historians. Pushing the pendulum back the other way, historians of the Progressive Era tended to commend the Jacksonians for the same things that Sumner, Catterall, and McGrane had deplored, especially when they construed phrases such as "the rich richer and the potent more powerful" as a Jacksonian attack on their own favorite target, free-market capitalism.[10]

Histories of Jacksonian banking thereby settled into their own stalemate around the question of whether Jackson's policies constituted a lost chance for American prosperity, until Arthur M. Schlesinger Jr. revisited the Bank War and Jacksonian economics in his epic work, *The Age of Jackson.* Writing at the end of the Second World War, Schlesinger saw in Jackson's times the same potential dangers as he saw in his own. In contrast to the Whiggish

patricians and Progressives, Schlesinger saw Jackson and his supporters as complex, with stronger intellectual ties to the East and
South than to the West. Instead of the disheveled minds of half-
educated frontiersmen, Schlesinger's Jacksonians were intelligent
and would shape the politics of their times with "much more reasoned and systematic notions about society than has been generally recognized." Schlesinger wanted to know how Americans
had solved the problem of reconciling completely opposed political ideologies without resorting to violent revolution. He saw important analogies between the philosophical conflicts of the Jacksonian era and those of his own emerging postwar world, and he
saw the conflict over the banking system as central, not only to
the early nineteenth century, but also to all of American history.
Schlesinger's Jacksonians were not asking, "Is there 'too much'
government?" Rather, they were asking, "Does the government
promote too much the interests of a single group?" Because no
event in American history better illustrated the problems related
to government size, activity, and special interests than the argument between the Whigs and the Jacksonians over the banking
system, Schlesinger came to see the defining event of the Jacksonian age as the defining issue in all of American history, which
he called the "irrepressible conflict of capitalism: the struggle on
the part of the business community to dominate the state, and on
the part of the rest of society, under the leadership of 'liberals,' to
check the political ambitions of business."[11]

Schlesinger brought his own revolution to Jacksonian historiography by realigning the conflicts of the period into class struggles instead of sectional conflicts. The most important "common
man" in Schlesinger's account, the eastern factory laborer, saw
in Jackson what, presumably, the farmers and factory workers of
Schlesinger's own time saw in Franklin D. Roosevelt. For Schlesinger, big business, not big government, represented the greatest
threat to liberty, and only a powerful government, itself governed
by an unwavering faith in free enterprise, could wield sufficient
strength to prevent powerful corporations from having their
way with democracy. Schlesinger interpreted the fight over the

banking system as a class-based struggle for the many advantages that accrued to one class or another once its representatives held power. He tended to read into the Jacksonians' ideas the issues with which his own generation had been most concerned and found evidence to support his interpretations precisely because he chose to make the Bank War the centerpiece of his account. Schlesinger provided the best concise explanation for Jacksonianism, the public-private structure of the BUS and the historical origins for both its support and its opposition. As Robert V. Remini has said, *The Age of Jackson* represents "the beginning of modern scholarship on Jackson and his era."[12]

Soon afterward, Richard Hofstadter took issue with Schlesinger's analysis by taking it a step further in his own deeply influential book, *The American Political Tradition and the Men Who Made It,* which is a series of small biographies of American statesmen. Hofstadter painted Jackson and his supporters as men on the make who assaulted the banking system not because they wanted to make opportunities for the common men who labored at the factory or the farm but because they hoped to turn it to their own benefit by strengthening the state banks at the expense of the national ones. Hofstadter attributed the Jacksonians' cynical ambitions to their desire not to be excluded from higher social circles, emphasizing the importance they placed on the status that economic prosperity would afford them rather than on pure economic advantage alone. The concept, which Hofstadter developed in later works as a tool for interpreting other social and political movements in American history, came to be known as "status politics." Hofstadter further argued that the Jacksonian era revealed more consensus than disagreement. All major players of the period, or any period in American history, had considered property rights and the right to free enterprise as sacred. The self-interested pursuit of property and opportunity, or the entrepreneurial spirit, had become the soul of the American political tradition, broadly accepted by most Americans and their leaders. In other words, "democracy" had come to mean the freedom to chase after a better social status and the privileges that came with it, or at least the right not to be excluded. Hofstadter thereby came to be associated with two other important interpretive tools used in American history, namely the "consensus" school and the "entrepreneurial thesis."[13]

Perhaps best argued by Bray Hammond, the entrepreneurial thesis gained currency as the best critical response to Schlesinger during the 1960s, and the consensus historians in general looked for ways to correct the progressives by emphasizing Americans' broad agreement on basic principles such as property rights and free enterprise. Taking the consensus view meant seeing the worst in the more radical movements from the American past, especially the Jacksonians and the Populists, who seemed in many ways to share Old Hickory's suspicion of financial institutions, even if they did not share his aversion to paper currency. Hammond therefore vigorously attacked the Jacksonians as greedy, would-be entrepreneurs who wrecked the BUS in order to open financial opportunities for themselves: Jackson's "conflict was not the traditionary one between the static rich and the static poor but a dynamic, revolutionary one between those who were already rich and those who sought to become rich." Armed with "the simple agrarian principles of political economy absorbed at his mother's knee" in one hand and "the most up-to-date doctrine of *laissez faire*" in the other, Jackson killed the BUS, but the fatal blow "was in no sense a blow at capitalism or property or the 'money power.' It was a blow at an older set of capitalists by a newer, more numerous set." Just as carefully as he had taken aim and cold-bloodedly killed Tennessee's best marksman, Charles Dickinson, in a duel, so had Jackson calculated his attack on Nicholas Biddle and the BUS.[14]

Jackson killed the bank, but Hammond wanted to show that the general had also broken with "the Hamiltonian concept of banking and the principle that supervision of banking as a monetary function was a responsibility of the federal government." Some of his constituents had wanted no banks at all, and some had wanted "more and more of them," so Jackson combined these irreconcilable views by destroying the central bank and replacing it with a profusion of state banks. As the Jacksonians went to war against the Bank, they claimed they were returning the nation to the ideal of free banking, which gave the right to establish a bank to anyone who would obey whatever banking rules had been established. Citizens in a democracy should not have to appease the money power in order to pursue entrepreneurship in the banking sector, argued the Jacksonians, even as Hammond wagged his finger at their catastrophic selfishness: "Free banking was the American democracy's choice of a permanent policy of monetary inflation—a policy that assures plenty of funds for all who wish to borrow, prices that rise in the long run persistently though haltingly, and a dollar that never ceases for long to shrink in value." Hammond's thesis combined Whiggish traditional views of Jackson with a Whiggish support for the use of a central bank to regulate smaller banks (known as the "sound banking doctrine") and, not surprisingly, resulted in the same Whiggish disgust for Jackson.[15]

Careful investigation revealed a significant weakness in Hammond's thesis, however. As Jean Alexander Wilburn showed in *Biddle's Bank: The Crucial Years,* the state banks of New York, at least, energetically supported the recharter of the BUS up until the time Jackson vetoed the recharter bill. James Roger Sharp took Hammond to task by using statistical sampling to examine the condition of state banks after the Panic of 1837, which the Jacksonian policies were supposed to have instigated. In his work *The Jacksonians versus the Banks: Politics in the States after the Panic of 1837,* Sharp divided the country into the larger sections, Southwest, Northwest, Northeast, and Southeast, and then took a representative state from each in order to provide "a nationwide survey of banking and politics on the state level after the Panic of 1837." Sharp chose 1837, because in that year the banks suspended specie payments and the Van Buren administration also abandoned the deposit bank system. He believed the effect "atomized the Bank War, thrusting the primary responsibility for the banking issue upon the states." The intervening years had given the new political parties time to define themselves and their differences more sharply, a purpose for which they had made great use of the banking controversies, so the cessation of specie payments and the end of the deposit system forced the parties to take determined stands on the issues, whereas in the earlier years, the parties had been "only temporary alliances of shifting coalitions."[16]

Sharp wanted to correct Hammond's argument that the Jacksonians, in their selfishness and ignorance, had nearly destroyed the American economy. Hammond had focused on the Bank War in isolation, not recognizing that the Democrats' campaign against banking and "the money power" continued in the states. "Although hard money Jacksonianism was based upon an anachronistic view of society and played upon the fears and antagonisms raised by a swiftly changing environment," acknowledged Sharp, "its legacy was a vital and enduring one." For Sharp, "the Democratic critique of the banking system after 1837, while not always translated into legislation, was still an important factor in making the banks more sensitive and responsible to public needs." All of the hard-money Jacksonians' demands for reform had as their bottom line "the restriction or elimination of the virtually unlimited power that ante-bellum bankers had over prices, the money supply, and the economic cycle." They demanded that banks have a broader base of specie upon which to issue notes, thus increasing the money supply, and that banks then be held to a fixed, limited percentage of their specie holdings for which they could in turn issue notes. If banks could not issue notes in irresponsible excess of their holdings in gold, reasoned the state-level Democrats, specie itself would, by its intrinsic value and inherent shortage, become "a kind of internal regulating device in the American banking system. The relatively stable and more responsible conduct of the country's banks from the early 1840s to the Civil War was due in large part to Democratic sponsored bank reforms and the vigorous hard-money critique."[17]

Sharp not only saw that the Jacksonians had better reasons for their policies than Hammond, Hofstadter, and other historians of the entrepreneurial and consensus schools had been willing to concede, but he also went against conventional wisdom by arguing that their ideas had worked. Jacksonian policies and the 1837 crisis had forced the "hards" and "softs" to work out an "uneasy consensus" that allowed for a steady expansion of credit self-regulated by the limitations of hard money yet sufficiently flexible to allow for steady expansion of credit that turned out to be more responsive to regional market demands and local supervision than the BUS had been. Sharp's Jacksonians were not "cynics but rather idealogues" who carried the banner for the deeply rooted conviction that paper money allowed bankers and their monied associates to manipulate the money supply and prices, which would lead to their gaining such political power that they could in turn give themselves special privileges and take away the liberties of others. Sharp's Jacksonians introduced in the early nineteenth century what the Greenbackers and Populists would try to accomplish by nearly opposite means at the end of the century: "Gain democratic control over banking." Finding logical reasons for each of the hard, soft, and Whig sides of Jacksonian banking enabled Sharp to move the field away from class struggle or lack thereof and toward a more naturally American exploration of the democratic principles at work and their interactions in politics.[18]

Historians Robert V. Remini, Harry L. Watson, and Charles G. Sellers Jr. followed with works that presented Jacksonian political, economic, and social ideals as integrated parts of a vastly more complex, complete world view. No one has written more on the Jacksonians than Remini, and his *Andrew Jackson and the Bank War: A Study in the Growth of Presidential Power* presents most of his views on the subject, but even he did not consider that he offered a radically new interpretation. "The Bank War used to be the most hotly disputed issue among Jacksonian historians," he wrote, "but so much was said about it in so concentrated a time span that everyone got pretty sick of it, even though the question of its meaning and importance was never resolved." Instead, he characterized himself as siding with Schlesinger. For Remini, the most interesting questions about the Bank War had less to do with whether the Jacksonians should be indicted for their treatment of the banks and more to do with Jackson himself and the ways his war on the BUS changed the presidency and U.S. political history.[19]

Through the Bank War, he contended, Jackson greatly increased the power of the executive branch. The veto message itself did not resemble the vetoes of any previous presidents, who had used the veto only sparingly and who had limited their messages to a discussion of the constitutionality of the bill in question. Remini observed that Jackson's arguments against the recharter of the BUS included forceful statements about the moral foundations of government and its role in the lives of citizens that gave his new Democratic Party the moral basis it needed to launch its crusade against the Whigs. Remini also believed that historians could not understand the era or the banking controversy unless they put Jackson in the place that Americans of the 1830s and 1840s put him: right in the middle of everything. Every major idea and movement of the period had Jackson as its reference, either for him or against him, so no one could hope to understand the period without putting Jackson's person—his example as a frontier success or backwoods demagogue—at the center.

Harry L. Watson and historians of somewhat similar persuasion, such as Joel Silbey and Sean Wilentz, have focused on the unique ways in which Jacksonian politics drew much of their emotional intensity from their application of morality to political problems. Combining Sellers's interest in the anxiety over the market revolution with Remini's attention to the fears over the threats to liberty posed by demagogues and strong governments alike, Watson saw in the Jacksonian economic discussion a "contest over the relationship between the emerging capitalist economy and the traditions of republican liberty and equality." Whigs saw the American System in particular and economic development in general as a national version of the moral and physical development society might expect from a young man, "growing in stature before God and man," as it were. For them, the Republic's promise could not be fulfilled without such growth, and those who stood in its way were at best hopeless troglodytes and at worst the cynical entrepreneurs that Hofstadter described. "Americans who had reason to fear or resent the progress of the industrial and commercial economy" could show their anger by voting for Jackson's campaign.[20]

Also in the early 1990s, Sellers published *The Market Revolution: Jacksonian America, 1815-1846*. Sellers extended George Rogers Taylor's highly influential 1951 analysis, *The Transportation Revolution, 1815-1860,* into a Marxist cultural critique. In his attempt to synthesize Jacksonian historiography, Sellers argued that as early as 1815 a market revolution was already under way. The revolution would eventually "fuel growth in countless ways, not least by providing the essential legal, financial, and transport infrastructures. Establishing capitalist hegemony over economy, politics, and culture, the market revolution created ourselves and most of the world we know." Railing against "our historiography of consensual, democratic capitalism" represented by Hofstadter, Hammond, and their consensus following, Sellers told the sad tale of a virtuous, agrarian Jeffersonian America overcome by a capitalist, bourgeois "hegemony." Two opposing modes of production, the land and the market, tore Jacksonian America apart and gave birth to its contradictions: slavery, racism, sexism, and elitism became more powerful even in the era that supposedly stood for reform, democracy, and the common man. Sellers blamed American cultural ills on the market revolution. Using the land to produce goods tended to root people in tradition, community, and family without excessive accumulation of wealth, because subsistence farming, by definition, did not allow the production of many extra goods that had value elsewhere after the basic needs for food, clothing, and shelter had been met. In contrast, producing for the market encouraged innovation, individualism, and competition to produce more goods that could be traded as items of value. As Americans of the Jacksonian era sought to participate in the market while holding on to their traditions, they found their families and communities torn apart by market forces that eventually revolutionized, or overturned, American society in ways even more profound than the transportation revolution.[21] Of course, Sellers has his critics. As Daniel Feller has recently pointed out, historians writing under the umbrella of Sellers's market revolution theory have not been able to produce much hard evidence, define the time period during which the revolution supposedly took place, or prove that the nation's transition to capitalism happened in Jackson's day instead of earlier, during the late colonial period.[22]

Given the dramatic financial events of 2008, the principles behind the old Jacksonian economic issues will likely return to public awareness. When they do, historians will need to ask better questions of the past in order to gain deeper insight into the complex questions of the present. Perhaps future generations of Jackson scholars will avoid asking dichotomous either/or questions that lead to the indictment or exoneration of Jackson and his policies. Perhaps they will instead look for ways to understand what that energetic, patriotic generation had to say to this generation's Whigs and Jacksonians. Doing so will require exploring the synergies between the many powerful themes that so energized the great war over the role of government.

NOTES

1. Andrew Jackson, "Veto Message," July 10, 1832, in *The Avalon Project at Yale Law School* (New Haven, Conn.: Lillian Goldman Law Library, 2005), http://avalon.law.yale.edu/. For my account of the Bank War, I am indebted to Robert V. Remini, *Andrew Jackson and the Bank War: A Study in the Growth of Presidential Power* (New York: Norton, 1967), and Daniel Feller's overview of the same in *The Jacksonian Promise: America, 1815-1840* (Baltimore: Johns Hopkins Univ. Press, 1995), 169-72.

2. Jackson, "Veto Message."

3. Ibid., 1-24; Harry L. Watson, *Liberty and Power: The Politics of Jacksonian America* (New York: Hill and Wang, 1990), 38-40; Murray N. Rothbard, *The Panic of 1819: Reactions and Policies* (New York: Columbia Univ. Press, 1962).

4. Andrew Jackson to Martin Van Buren, Aug. 16, 1833, in *The Correspondence of Andrew Jackson,* ed. John Spencer Bassett, 6 vols. (Washington, D.C.: Carnegie Institution of Washington, 1926-33), 5:159.

5. Jackson, "Veto Message."

6. Ibid.

7. Ibid.

8. Jackson to Andrew Jackson Jr., Oct. 11, 1833, in *Correspondence of Andrew Jackson,* ed. Bassett, 5:217.

9. William Graham Sumner, *A History of American Currency, with Chapters on the English Bank Restriction and Austrian Paper Money* (New York: H. Holt, 1874); Sumner, *Andrew Jackson as a Public Man: What He Was, What Chances He Had, and What He Did with Them* (1882; Boston: Houghton Mifflin, 1910), 349.

10. Ralph C. H. Catterall, *The Second Bank of the United States* (Chicago: Univ. of Chicago Press, 1903); Reginald Charles McGrane, *The Panic of 1837: Some Financial Problems of the Jacksonian Era* (Chicago: Univ. of Chicago Press, 1924).

11. Arthur M. Schlesinger Jr., *The Age of Jackson* (Boston: Little, Brown, and Co., 1945), x, 415.

12. Robert V. Remini, *The Jacksonian Era* (Arlington Heights, Ill.: H. Davidson, 1989), 130.

13. Richard Hofstadter, *The American Political Tradition and the Men Who Made It* (New York: Alfred A. Knopf, 1948).

14. Bray Hammond, *Banks and Politics in America: From the Revolution to the Civil War* (Princeton, N.J.: Princeton Univ. Press, 1957), 349, 328. Hammond used *laisser faire,* which is the infinitive form of the verb usually used in English-language histories in its imperative form, *laissez faire.* The phrase first appeared in English in the 1820s and is therefore itself a historical artifact pointing to the trans-Atlantic nature of the debate over the proper role of government in the economy. The phrase means "to let do" and was used in France by eighteenth-century French economists who wanted to promote free trade. Hammond may only have been showing off his French, however.

15. Ibid., 573.

16. Jean Alexander Wilburn, *Biddle's Bank: The Crucial Years* (New York: Columbia Univ. Press, 1967); James Roger Sharp, *The Jacksonians versus the Banks: Politics in the States after the Panic of 1837* (New York: Columbia Univ. Press, 1970), x.

17. Sharp, *Jacksonians versus the Banks,* 328-29, 8.

18. Ibid., viii, 5.

19. Robert V. Remini, *Andrew Jackson and the Bank War: A Study in the Growth of Presidential Power* (New York: Norton, 1967); Remini, *The Revolutionary Age of Andrew Jackson* (New York: Harper and Row, 1976), 189.

20. Watson, *Liberty and Power,* 171.

21. Charles G. Sellers Jr., *The Market Revolution: Jacksonian America, 1815-1846* (New York: Oxford Univ. Press, 1991), 5; George Rogers Taylor, *The Transportation Revolution, 1815-1860* (New York: Rinehart, 1951). See also Sellers, "Andrew Jackson versus the Historians," *Mississippi Valley Historical Review* 44 (Mar. 1958): 615-34.

22. Daniel Feller, "Rediscovering Jacksonian America," in *The State of U.S. History,* ed. Melvyn Stokes (New York: Berg, 2002), 69-92.

Bibliography

ARCHIVES

Boston Public Library
Miller Center for Public Affairs, University of Virginia

PRIMARY AND SECONDARY SOURCES

Abel, Annie Heloise. *The History of Events Resulting in Indian Consolidation West of the Mississippi.* Washington, D.C.: American Historical Association, 1908.

Abernethy, Thomas P. *From Frontier to Plantation in Tennessee: A Study in Frontier Democracy.* Chapel Hill: University of North Carolina Press, 1932. Reprint, Tuscaloosa: University of Alabama Press, 1967.

Abzug, Robert H. *Cosmos Crumbling: American Reform and the Religious Imagination.* New York: Oxford University Press, 1994.

Akers, Dona L. "Removing the Heart of the Choctaw People: Indian Removal from the Native Perspective." *American Indian Culture and Research Journal* 23 (Summer 1999): 63-76.

Altschuler, Glenn. "Democracy as a Work in Progress." *Reviews in American History* 34 (June 2006): 169-75.

American Anti-Slavery Society. *Proceedings of the American Anti-Slavery Society at Its Third Decade, Held in the City of Philadelphia, Dec. 3d and 4th, 1863.* New York: American Anti-Slavery Society, 1864.

American Temperance Union. *Permanent Temperance Documents of the American Temperance Society.* New York: American Temperance Union, 1843.

Anbinder, Tyler. *Nativism and Slavery: The Northern Know Nothings and the Politics of the 1850s.* New York: Oxford University Press, 1992.

Andrews, John A. *From Revivals to Removal: Jeremiah Evarts, the Cherokee Nation, and the Search for the Soul of America.* Athens: University of Georgia Press, 1992.

Anson, Bert. "Variations of the Indian Conflict: The Effects of the Emigrant Indian Removal Policy, 1830-1854." *Missouri Historical Review* 59 (October 1964): 64-89.

Ashworth, John. *Slavery, Capitalism, and Politics in the Antebellum Republic.* Vol. 1, *Commerce and Compromise, 1820-1850.* Cambridge: Cambridge University Press, 1995.

Atkins, Jonathan M. *Parties, Politics, and the Sectional Conflict in Tennessee, 1832-1861.* Knoxville: University of Tennessee Press, 1997.

Bailyn, Bernard. *The Ideological Origins of the American Revolution.* Cambridge, Mass.: Belknap Press of Harvard University Press, 1967.

Baker, Jean. *Votes for Women: The Struggle for Suffrage Revisited.* New York: Oxford University Press, 2002.

Banner, James M., Jr. "The Problem of South Carolina." In *The Hofstadter Aegis: A Memorial,* edited by Stanley Elkins and Eric McKitrick, 60-93. New York: Alfred A. Knopf, 1974.

Banning, Lance. *The Jeffersonian Persuasion.* Ithaca, N.Y.: Cornell University Press, 1978.

Barney, William L. *The Passage of the Republic: An Interdisciplinary History of Nineteenth-Century America.* Lexington, Mass.: DC Heath and Company, 1987.

Bassett, John Spencer, ed. *The Correspondence of Andrew Jackson.* 6 vols. Washington, D.C.: Carnegie Institution of Washington, 1926-33.

———. *The Life of Andrew Jackson.* New York: Macmillan, 1916.

Beecher, Lyman. *Six Sermons on the Nature, Occasions, Signs, Evils, and Remedy of Intemperance.* New York: American Tract Society, 1827.

Benson, Lee. *The Concept of Jacksonian Democracy: New York as a Test Case.* Princeton, N.J.: Princeton University Press, 1961.

Blight, David W. *Frederick Douglass' Civil War: Keeping Faith in Jubilee.* Baton Rouge: Louisiana State University Press, 1989.

Bollwerk, Elizabeth. "Controlling Acculturation: A Potawatomi Strategy for Avoiding Removal." *Midcontinental Journal of Archaeology* 32, no. 1 (2006): 117-41.

Booraem, Hendrik. *Young Hickory: The Making of Andrew Jackson.* Dallas, Tex.: Taylor, 2001.

Boylan, Anne M. *The Origins of Women's Activism: New York and Boston, 1797-1840.* Chapel Hill: University of North Carolina Press, 2002.

Brands, H. W. *Andrew Jackson: His Life and Times.* New York: Doubleday, 2005.

Brown, Richard D. *Modernization: The Transformation of American Life, 1600-1865.* New York: Hill and Wang, 1976.

Burin, Eric. *Slavery and the Peculiar Solution: A History of the American Colonization Society.* Gainesville: University Press of Florida, 2005.

Burke, Joseph C. "The Cherokee Cases: A Study in Law, Politics, and Morality." *Stanford Law Review* 21 (February 1969): 500-531.

Burstein, Andrew. *America's Jubilee, July 4, 1826: A Generation Remembers the Revolution after Fifty Years of Independence.* New York: Vintage, 2001.

———. *The Passions of Andrew Jackson.* New York: Knopf, 2003.

Capers, Gerald M. *John C. Calhoun: Opportunist; A Reappraisal.* Chicago: Quadrangle Books, 1969.

Carlson, Douglas. "'Drinks He to His Own Undoing': Temperance Ideology in the Deep South." *Journal of the Early Republic* 18 (1998): 659-91.

Carson, James Taylor. "State Rights and Indian Removal in Mississippi, 1817-1835." *Journal of Mississippi History* 57, no. 1 (1995): 25-41.

Catterall, Ralph C. H. *The Second Bank of the United States.* Chicago: University of Chicago Press, 1903.

Cave, Alfred A. "Abuse of Power: Andrew Jackson and the Indian Removal Act of 1830." *Historian* 64, no. 6 (2002): 1330-53.

———. *Jacksonian Democracy and the Historians.* Gainesville: University of Florida Press, 1964.

Cayton, Andrew R. L. *The Frontier Republic: Ideology and Politics in the Ohio Country, 1780-1825.* Kent, Ohio: Kent State University Press, 1986.

Chambers, William Nisbet, and Walter Dean Burnham, eds., *The American Party Systems: Stages of Political Development.* New York: Oxford University Press, 1967.

Cheathem, Mark R. *Old Hickory's Nephew: The Political and Private Struggles of Andrew Jackson Donelson.* Baton Rouge: Louisiana State University Press, 2007.

Clark, Christopher. "The Consequences of the Market Revolution in the American North." In *The Market Revolution in America: Social, Political, and Religious Expressions, 1800-1880,* edited by Melvyn Stokes and Stephen Conway, 23-42. Charlottesville: University Press of Virginia, 1996.

———. *The Roots of Rural Capitalism: Western Massachusetts, 1780-1860.* Ithaca, N.Y.: Cornell University Press, 1990.

Coit, Margaret L. *John C. Calhoun: American Portrait.* Southern Classics Series. 1950. Columbia: University of South Carolina Press, 1991.

Cole, Donald B. *Jacksonian Democracy in New Hampshire, 1800-1851.* Cambridge, Mass.: Harvard University Press, 1970.

———. *The Presidency of Andrew Jackson.* Lawrence: University Press of Kansas, 1993.

Conn, Steven. *History's Shadow: Native Americans and Historical Consciousness in the Nineteenth Century.* Chicago: University of Chicago Press, 2004.

Cooper, William J., Jr. *The South and the Politics of Slavery, 1828-1856.* Baton Rouge: Louisiana State University Press, 1978.

Crofts, Daniel W. *Old Southampton: Politics and Society in a Virginia County, 1834-1869.* Charlottesville: University Press of Virginia, 1992.

Cross, Whitney R. *The Burned-over District: The Social and Intellectual History of Enthusiastic Religion in Western New York, 1800-1850.* Ithaca, N.Y.: Cornell University Press, 1950.

Curtis, James C. *Andrew Jackson and the Search for Vindication.* New York: HarperCollins, 1976.

DeRosier, Arthur H., Jr. *The Removal of the Choctaw Indians.* Knoxville: University of Tennessee Press, 1970.

Dillon, Merton. "The Failure of the American Abolitionists." *Journal of Southern History* 25, no. 2 (1959): 159-77.

Dillon, Merton L. "The Abolitionists: A Decade of Historiography, 1959-1969." *Journal of Southern History* 35, no. 4 (1969): 500-522.

Dixon, Chris. *Perfecting the Family: Antislavery Marriages in Nineteenth-Century America.* Amherst: University of Massachusetts Press, 1997.

Dorsey, Bruce. *Reforming Men and Women: Gender in the Antebellum City.* Ithaca, N.Y.: Cornell University Press, 2002.

Downey, Tom. *Planting a Capitalist South: Masters, Merchants, and Manufacturers in the Southern Interior, 1790-1860.* Baton Rouge: Louisiana State University Press, 2005.

Dublin, Thomas. *Transforming Women's Work: New England Lives in the Industrial Revolution.* Ithaca, N.Y.: Cornell University Press, 1994.

DuBois, Ellen. "Women's Rights and Abolition: The Nature of the Connection." In *Antislavery Reconsidered: New Perspectives on the Abolitionists,* edited by Lewis Perry and Michael Fellman, 238-51. Baton Rouge: Louisiana State University Press, 1979.

DuBois, Ellen Carol. *Feminism and Suffrage: The Emergence of an Independent Women's Movement in America, 1848-1869.* Ithaca, N.Y.: Cornell University Press, 1978.

Dupre, Daniel. *Transforming the Cotton Frontier: Madison County, Alabama, 1800-1840.* Baton Rouge: Louisiana State University Press, 1997.

Eby, Cecil. *"That Disgraceful Affair": The Black Hawk War.* New York: W. W. Norton and Company, 1973.

Ellis, Richard. *The Jeffersonian Crisis: Courts and Politics in the Young Republic.* New York: Oxford University Press, 1971.

———. "The Market Revolution and the Transformation of American Politics, 1801-1837." In *The Market Revolution in America: Social, Political, and Religious Expressions, 1800-1880,* edited by Melvyn Stokes and Stephen Conway, 149-76. Charlottesville: University Press of Virginia, 1996.

Ellis, Richard E. *The Union at Risk: Jacksonian Democracy, States' Rights and the Nullification Crisis.* New York: Oxford University Press, 1987.

Ericson, David F. "The Nullification Crisis, American Republicanism, and the Force Bill Debate." *Journal of Southern History* 61 (May 1995): 249-70.

———. *The Shaping of American Liberalism: The Debates over Ratification, Nullification, and Slavery.* Chicago: University of Chicago Press, 1993.

Feller, Daniel. *The Jacksonian Promise: America, 1815-1840.* Baltimore: Johns Hopkins University Press, 1995.

———. "The Market Revolution Ate My Homework." *Reviews in American History* 25 (September 1997): 408-15.

———. "Politics and Society: Toward a Jacksonian Synthesis." *Journal of the Early Republic* 10 (Summer 1990): 135-61.

———. "Rediscovering Jacksonian America." In *The State of U.S. History,* edited by Melvyn Stokes, 69-91. Oxford: Berg, 2002.

Fletcher, Holly Berkley. *Gender and the American Temperance Movement of the Nineteenth Century.* New York: Routledge, 2008.

Foner, Eric. *Free Soil, Free Labor, Free Men: The Ideology of the Republican Party before the Civil War.* New York: Oxford University Press, 1970.

Ford, Lacy K., Jr. "Inventing the Concurrent Majority: Madison, Calhoun, and the Problem of Majoritarianism in American Political Thought." *Journal of Southern History* 60 (February 1994): 19-58.

———. *Origins of Southern Radicalism: The South Carolina Upcountry, 1800-1860.* New York: Oxford University Press, 1988.

———. "Republican Ideology in a Slave Society: The Political Economy of John C. Calhoun." *Journal of Southern History* 54 (August 1988): 405-24.

Foreman, Grant. *Indian Removal: The Emigration of the Five Civilized Tribes.* Norman: University of Oklahoma Press, 1932.

———. *The Last Trek of the Indians.* Chicago: University of Chicago Press, 1946.

Formisano, Ronald P. *The Birth of Mass Political Parties: Michigan, 1827-1861.* Princeton, N.J.: Princeton University Press, 1971.

———. *For the People: American Populist Movements from the Revolution to the 1850s.* Chapel Hill: University of North Carolina Press, 2007.

———. "Political Character, Antipartyism, and the Second Party System." *American Quarterly* 21 (1969): 683-709.

Freehling, William. *Prelude to Civil War: The Nullification Controversy in South Carolina, 1816-1836.* New York: Oxford University Press, 1965.

Friend, Craig Thompson. *Along The Maysville Road: The Early American Republic in the Trans-Appalachian West.* Knoxville: University of Tennessee Press, 2005.

Garrison, Tim Alan. *The Legal Ideology of Removal: The Southern Judiciary and the Sovereignty of Native American Nations.* Athens: University of Georgia Press, 2002.

Garvey, T. Gregory. *Creating the Culture of Reform in Antebellum America.* Athens: University of Georgia Press, 2006.

Ginzberg, Lori D. *Women and the Work of Benevolence: Morality, Politics, and Class in the Nineteenth-Century United States.* New Haven, Conn.: Yale University Press, 1990.

Gray, Susan E. "Limits and Possibilities: White-Indian Relations in Western Michigan in the Era of Removal." *Michigan Historical Review* 20, no. 3 (1994): 71-91.

Green, Michael. *The Politics of Indian Removal.* Lincoln: University of Nebraska Press, 1982.

Grimké, Angelina E. *Letters to Catherine E. Beecher, in Reply to an Essay on Slavery and Abolitionism, Addressed to A. E. Grimké, Revised by the Author.* Boston: Isaac Knapp, 1838.

Grimké, Sarah M. *Letters on the Equality of the Sexes and the Condition of Women, Addressed to Mary S. Parker, President of the Boston Female Anti-Slavery Society.* Boston: Isaac Knapp, 1838.

Grob, Gerald N., and George Athan Billias, eds. *Interpretations of American History: Patterns and Perspectives.* Vol. 1, *To 1877.* 6th ed. New York: Free Press, 1992.

Guttman, Allen. *States' Rights and Indian Removal: The Cherokee Nation versus the State of Georgia.* Washington, D.C.: DC Heath, 1964.

Hallowell, Anna Davis, ed. *James and Lucretia Mott: Life and Letters.* Boston: Houghton, Mifflin and Co., 1884.

Hammond, Bray. *Banks and Politics in America: From the Revolution to the Civil War.* Princeton, N.J.: Princeton University Press, 1957.

———. Review of *The Age of Jackson,* by Arthur M. Schlesinger Jr. *Journal of Economic History* 6 (May 1946): 79-84.

Hartz, Louis. *The Liberal Tradition in America: An Interpretation of American Political Thought since the Revolution.* New York: Harcourt, Brace, 1955.

Hershberger, Mary. "Mobilizing Women, Anticipating Abolition: The Struggle against Indian Removal in the 1830s." *Journal of American History* 86 (June 1999): 15-40.

Hersh, Blanche Glassman. "'Am I Not a Woman and a Sister?': Abolitionist Beginnings of Nineteenth-Century Feminism." In *Antislavery Reconsidered: New Perspectives on the Abolitionists,* edited by Lewis Perry and Michael Fellman, 252-83. Baton Rouge: Louisiana State University Press, 1979.

Hofstadter, Richard. *The American Political Tradition and the Men Who Made It.* New York: Knopf, 1948.

Holt, Michael. *The Rise and Fall of the American Whig Party: Jacksonian Politics and the Onset of the Civil War.* Oxford: Oxford University Press, 1999.

Holt, Michael F. "The Anti-Masonic and Know Nothing Parties." In *History of U.S. Political Parties,* edited by Arthur M. Schlesinger Jr., vol. 1, 575-620. New York: Chelsea House, 1973.

———. *Political Parties and American Political Development: From the Age of Jackson to the Age of Lincoln.* Baton Rouge: Louisiana State University Press, 1992.

Howe, Daniel Walker. *The Political Culture of the American Whigs.* Chicago: University of Chicago Press, 1979.

———. *What Hath God Wrought: The Transformation of America, 1815-1848.* Oxford: Oxford University Press, 2006.

Hugins, Walter. *Jacksonian Democracy and the Working Class: A Study of the New York Workingmen's Movement, 1829-1837.* Palo Alto, Calif., Stanford University Press, 1960.

Huston, Reeve. *Land and Freedom: Rural Society, Popular Protest, and Party Politics in Antebellum New York.* New York: Oxford University Press, 2000.

Isenberg, Nancy. *Sex and Citizenship in Antebellum America.* Chapel Hill: University of North Carolina Press, 1998.

Jackson, Andrew. "Veto Message," July 10, 1832. In *The Avalon Project at Yale Law School.* New Haven, Conn.: Lillian Goldman Law Library, 2005.

Jeffrey, Julie Roy. *The Great Silent Army of Abolitionism: Ordinary Women in the Antislavery Movement.* Chapel Hill: University of North Carolina Press, 1998.

Johnson, Paul. *The Early American Republic, 1789-1829.* New York: Oxford University Press, 2007.

Johnson, Reinhard O. *The Liberty Party, 1840-1848: Antislavery Third-Party Politics in the United States.* Baton Rouge: Louisiana State University Press, 2009.

Kelley, Robert. *The Cultural Pattern of American Politics: The First Century.* New York: Knopf, 1979.

Kerber, Linda. *Federalists in Dissent: Ideology and Imagery in Jeffersonian America.* Ithaca, N.Y.: Cornell University Press, 1970.

Kerber, Linda K. "Separate Spheres, Female Worlds, Woman's Place: The Rhetoric of Women's History." *Journal of American History* 75, no. 1 (1988): 9-39.

Keyssar, Alexander. *The Right to Vote: The Contested History of Democracy in the United States.* New York: Basic Books, 2000.

Kraut, Alan M. *Crusaders and Compromisers: Essays on the Relationship of the Antislavery Struggle to the Antebellum Party System.* Westport, Conn.: Greenwood Press, 1983.

Kruman, Marc W. *Parties and Politics in North Carolina, 1836-1865.* Baton Rouge: Louisiana State University Press, 1983.

———. "The Second American Party System and the Transformation of Revolutionary Republicanism." *Journal of the Early Republic* 12 (1992): 509-37.

Lancaster, Jane F. *Removal Aftershock: The Seminoles' Struggle to Survive in the West, 1836-1866*. Knoxville: University of Tennessee Press, 1994.

Larson, John. *Internal Improvement: National Public Works and the Promise of Popular Government in the Early United States*. Chapel Hill: University of North Carolina Press, 2001.

Latner, Richard B. *The Presidency of Andrew Jackson, 1829-1837*. Athens: University of Georgia Press, 1982.

Leonard, Gerald. *The Invention of Party Politics: Federalism, Popular Sovereignty, and Constitutional Developments in Jacksonian Illinois*. Chapel Hill: University of North Carolina Press, 2002.

———. "The Ironies of Partyism and Antipartyism: Origins of Partisan Political Culture in Jacksonian Illinois." *Illinois Historical Journal* 87 (Spring 1994): 21-40.

Lewis, Jan Ellen. "What We Talk about When We Talk about Democracy." *Journal of the Historical Society* 6 (December 2006): 527-36.

Litwack, Leon. *North of Slavery: The Negro in the Free States, 1790-1860*. Chicago: University of Chicago Press, 1961.

Lovell, Laura H. *Report of a Delegate to the Anti-Slavery Convention of American Women. Held in Philadelphia, May, 1838*. Boston: J. Knapp, 1838.

Mahon, John K. *History of the Second Seminole War, 1835-1842*. Gainesville: University of Florida Press, 1967.

Maier, Pauline. "The Road Not Taken: Nullification, John C. Calhoun, and the Revolutionary Tradition in South Carolina." *South Carolina Historical Magazine* 82 (1981): 1-19.

Martin, Scott C. *Devil of the Domestic Sphere: Temperance, Gender, and Middle-Class Ideology, 1800-1860*. Dekalb: Northern Illinois University Press, 2008.

Massachusetts Female Emancipation Society. *First Annual Report of the Massachusetts Female Emancipation Society*. Boston: James Loring, 1841.

Mayer, Henry. *All on Fire: William Lloyd Garrison and the Abolition of Slavery*. New York: St. Martin's Press, 1998.

May, Samuel J. *Some Recollections of Our Antislavery Conflict*. Boston: Fields, Osgood, and Co., 1869.

McCarthy, Timothy Patrick, and John Stauffer. *Prophets of Protest: Reconsidering the History of American Abolitionism*. New York: New Press, distributed by W. W. Norton, 2006.

McCormick, Richard P. "New Perspectives on Jacksonian Politics." *American Historical Review* 65 (January 1960): 288-301.

————. *The Second American Party System: Party Formation in the Jacksonian Era.* Chapel Hill: University of North Carolina Press, 1966.

McCoy, Drew. *The Elusive Republic: Political Economy in Jeffersonian America.* Chapel Hill: Published for the Institute of Early American History and Culture, Williamsburg, Va., by the University of North Carolina Press, 1980.

McGrane, Reginald Charles. *The Panic of 1837: Some Financial Problems of the Jacksonian Era.* Chicago: University of Chicago Press, 1924.

McKivigan, John R., and Stanley Harrold. *Antislavery Violence: Sectional, Racial, and Cultural Conflict in Antebellum America.* Knoxville: University of Tennessee Press, 1999.

McMillen, Sally Gregory. *Seneca Falls and the Origins of the Women's Rights Movement.* New York: Oxford University Press, 2008.

McPherson, James M. *The Abolitionist Legacy: From Reconstruction to the NAACP.* Princeton, N.J.: Princeton University Press, 1975.

Melder, Keith E. *Beginnings of Sisterhood: The American Woman's Rights Movement, 1800–1850.* New York: Schocken Books, 1977.

Meyers, Marvin. *The Jacksonian Persuasion: Politics and Belief.* Palo Alto, Calif., Stanford University Press, 1957.

Minges, Patrick. "Beneath the Underdog: Race, Religion, and the Trail of Tears." *American Indian Quarterly* 25, no. 3 (2001): 453–79.

Mintz, Steven. *Moralists and Modernizers: America's Pre-Civil War Reformers.* Baltimore: Johns Hopkins University Press, 1995.

Moser, Harold, ed. *The Papers of Andrew Jackson.* Vol. 6, *1825–1828.* Knoxville: University of Tennessee Press, 2002.

Newman, Richard S. *The Transformation of American Abolitionism: Fighting Slavery in the Early Republic.* Chapel Hill: University of North Carolina Press, 2002.

Newman, Simon. *Parades and the Politics of the Street: Festive Culture in the Early American Republic.* Philadelphia: University of Pennsylvania Press, 1997.

Niven, John. *John C. Calhoun and the Price of Union.* Baton Rouge: Louisiana State University Press, 1988.

Oakes, James. "The Age of Jackson and the Rise of American Democracies." *Journal of the Historical Society* 6 (December 2006): 491–500.

Ogg, Frederick A. *The Reign of Andrew Jackson.* New Haven, Conn.: Yale University Press, 1919.

Parton, James. *Life of Andrew Jackson.* 3 vols. New York: Mason Brothers, 1861.

"Pastoral Letter." *Genius of Universal Emancipation,* August 11, 1837.

Pierson, Michael D. *Free Hearts and Free Homes: Gender and American Antislavery Politics.* Chapel Hill: University of North Carolina Press, 2003.

Perry, Lewis, and Michael Fellman. *Antislavery Reconsidered: New Perspectives on the Abolitionists.* Baton Rouge: Louisiana State University Press, 1979.

Peskin, Lawrence A. "How the Republicans Learned to Love Manufacturing: The First Parties and the 'New Economy.'" *Journal of the Early Republic* 22 (Summer 2002): 235-62.

Pessen, Edward. *Jacksonian America: Society, Personality, and Politics.* Rev. ed. Urbana: University of Illinois Press, 1985.

———. Review of *The Market Revolution: Jacksonian America, 1815-1846,* by Charles Sellers. *Journal of Southern History* 59 (November 1993): 750-52.

Peterson, Merrill D. *The Great Triumvirate: Webster, Clay, and Calhoun.* New York: Oxford University Press, 1987.

Pillsbury, Parker. *Acts of the Anti-Slavery Apostles.* Concord, N.H.: Clague, Wegman, Schlict, 1883.

Pocock, J. G. A. *The Machiavellian Moment: Florentine Political Thought and the Atlantic Republican Tradition.* Princeton, N.J.: Princeton University Press, 1975.

Prucha, Francis Paul. "Andrew Jackson's Indian Policy: A Reassessment." *Journal of American History* 56 (1969): 527-39.

Quist, John W. *Restless Visionaries: The Social Roots of Antebellum Reform in Alabama and Michigan.* Baton Rouge: Louisiana State University Press, 1998.

Ratcliffe, Donald J. "The Nullification Crisis, Southern Discontents, and the American Political Process." *American Nineteenth Century History* 1 (2000): 1-30.

———. *The Politics of Long Division: The Birth of the Second Party System in Ohio, 1818-1828.* Columbus: Ohio State University Press, 2000.

Ray, Kristofer. *Middle Tennessee, 1775-1825: Progress and Popular Democracy on the Southwestern Frontier.* Knoxville: University of Tennessee Press, 2007.

Remini, Robert V. *Andrew Jackson and the Bank War: A Study in the Growth of Presidential Power.* New York: Norton, 1967.

———. *Andrew Jackson and the Course of American Democracy.* New York: Harper and Row, 1984.

———. *Andrew Jackson and the Course of American Empire.* New York: Harper and Row, 1977.

———. *Andrew Jackson and the Course of American Freedom.* New York: Harper and Row, 1981.

———. *Henry Clay: Statesman for the Union.* New York: W. W. Norton, 1991.

———. *The Jacksonian Era.* Arlington Heights, Ill.: H. Davidson, 1989.

———. *John Quincy Adams.* New York: Times Books, 2002.

———. *The Legacy of Andrew Jackson: Essays on Democracy, Indian Removal, and Slavery.* Baton Rouge: Louisiana State University Press, 1988.

——. *The Revolutionary Age of Andrew Jackson*. New York: Harper and Row, 1976.

Richards, Leonard L. *Gentlemen of Property and Standing: Anti-Abolition Mobs in Jacksonian America*. New York: Oxford University Press, 1970.

Rogin, Michael Paul. *Fathers and Children: Andrew Jackson and the Subjugation of the American Indian*. New York: Knopf, 1975. Reprint, New Brunswick, N.J.: Transaction, 1991.

Rose, Anne C. *Voices of the Marketplace: American Thought and Culture, 1830-1860*. New York: Twayne, 1995.

Rothbard, Murray N. *The Panic of 1819: Reactions and Policies*. New York: Columbia University Press, 1962.

Ryan, Mary P. *Women in Public: Between Banners and Ballots, 1825-1880*. Baltimore: Johns Hopkins University Press, 1990.

Ryan, Susan M. *The Grammar of Good Intentions: Race and the Antebellum Culture of Benevolence*. Ithaca, N.Y.: Cornell University Press, 2005.

Salerno, Beth. *Sister Societies: Women's Antislavery Organizations in Antebellum America*. DeKalb: Northern Illinois University Press, 2005.

Satz, Ronald N. *American Indian Policy in the Jacksonian Era*. Lincoln: University of Nebraska Press, 1975.

Schlesinger, Arthur M., Jr. *The Age of Jackson*. New York: Little, Brown, 1945.

——. *The Imperial Presidency*. Boston: Houghton Mifflin, 1973.

——. "The States' Rights Fetish." In *New Viewpoints in American History*, 220-44. New York: Macmillan, 1922.

Sellers, Charles. *The Market Revolution: Jacksonian America, 1815-1846*. Oxford: Oxford University Press, 1991.

Sellers, Charles G., Jr. "Andrew Jackson versus the Historians." *Mississippi Valley Historical Review* 44 (March 1958): 615-34.

Sewell, Richard H. *Ballots for Freedom: Antislavery Politics in the United States, 1837-1860*. New York: W. W. Norton and Company, 1976.

Shade, William G. *Banks or No Banks: The Money Issue in Western Politics, 1832-1865*. Detroit: Wayne State University Press, 1972.

——. *Democratizing the Old Dominion: Virginia and the Second Party System, 1824-1861*. Charlottesville: University Press of Virginia, 1996.

——. Review of *The Market Revolution: Jacksonian America, 1815-1846*, by Charles Sellers. *Journal of Economic History* 53 (June 1993): 429-30.

Shankman, Andrew. *Crucible of American Democracy: The Struggle to Fuse Egalitarianism and Capitalism in Jeffersonian Pennsylvania*. Lawrence: University Press of Kansas, 2004.

Sharp, James Roger. *The Jacksonians versus the Banks: Politics in the States after the Panic of 1837*. New York: Columbia University Press, 1970.

Silbey, Joel H. *The American Political Nation, 1838-1893*. Palo Alto, Calif., Stanford University Press, 1991.

Sklar, Kathryn Kish. "Women Who Speak for an Entire Nation." In *The Abolitionist Sisterhood: Women's Political Culture in Antebellum America,* edited by Jean Fagan Yellin and John C. Van Horne, 301-33. Ithaca, N.Y.: Cornell University Press, 1994.

Sklar, Kathryn Kish, and James Brewer Stewart. *Women's Rights and Transatlantic Antislavery in the Era of Emancipation.* New Haven, Conn.: Yale University Press, 2007.

Stanton, Elizabeth Cady, Susan B. Anthony, and Matilda Joslyn Gage. *History of Woman Suffrage.* Vol. 1. 1881. New York: Arno Press, 1969.

Stauffer, John. *The Black Hearts of Men: Radical Abolitionists and the Transformation of Race.* Cambridge, Mass.: Harvard University Press, 2002.

Stewart, James Brewer. *Holy Warriors: The Abolitionists and American Slavery.* Rev. ed. New York: Hill and Wang, 1996.

Stokes, Melvyn, and Stephen Conway, eds. *The Market Revolution in America: Social, Political, and Religious Expressions, 1800-1880.* Charlottesville: University Press of Virginia, 1996.

Sumner, William Graham. *Andrew Jackson as a Public Man: What He Was, What Chances He Had, and What He Did with Them.* 1882. Boston: Houghton Mifflin, 1910.

———. *A History of American Currency, with Chapters on the English Bank Restriction and Austrian Paper Money.* New York: H. Holt, 1874.

"A Symposium on Charles Sellers, *The Market Revolution: Jacksonian America, 1815-1846.*" *Journal of the Early Republic* 12 (Winter 1992): 445-76.

Taylor, George Rogers. *The Transportation Revolution, 1815-1860.* New York: Rinehart, 1951.

Terborg-Penn, Rosalyn. *African American Women in the Struggle for the Vote, 1850-1920.* Bloomington: Indiana University Press, 1998.

Thornton, J. Mills, III. *Politics and Power in a Slave Society: Alabama, 1800-1860.* Baton Rouge: Louisiana State University Press, 1978.

de Tocqueville, Alexis. *Democracy in America.* Edited by J. P. Mayer and translated by George Lawrence. New York: Perennial, 2000.

Turner, Frederick Jackson. *The Frontier in American History.* 1920. Reprint, New York: Henry Holt, 1953.

Van Deusen, Glyndon G. *The Jacksonian Era, 1828-1848.* New York: Harper and Brothers, 1959.

Van Every, Dale. *Disinherited: The Lost Birthright of the American Indian.* New York: Morrow and Company, 1966.

Varon, Elizabeth R. *We Mean to Be Counted: White Women and Politics in Antebellum Virginia.* Chapel Hill: University of North Carolina, 1998.

Vorenberg, Michael. *Final Freedom: The Civil War, the Abolition of Slavery, and the Thirteenth Amendment.* New York: Cambridge University Press, 2001.

Voss-Hubbard, Mark. *Beyond Party: Cultures of Antipartisanship in Northern Politics before the Civil War.* Baltimore: Johns Hopkins University Press, 2002.

Wallace, Anthony F. C. *The Long, Bitter Trail: Andrew Jackson and the Indians.* New York: Hill and Wang, 1993.

Walters, Ronald G. *American Reformers, 1815-1860.* New York: Hill and Wang, 1978.

Ward, John William. *Andrew Jackson: Symbol for an Age.* New York: Oxford University Press, 1955.

Warren, Kim. "Separate Spheres: Analytical Persistence in United States Women's History." *History Compass* 5, no. 1 (2007): 262-77.

Warshauer, Matthew S. Review of *The Passions of Andrew Jackson,* by Andrew Burstein. *Tennessee Historical Quarterly* 63 (Winter 2003): 366-73.

Watson, Harry L., ed. *Andrew Jackson vs. Henry Clay: Democracy and Development in Antebellum America.* Boston: Bedford/St. Martin, 1998.

———. *Jacksonian Politics and Community Conflict: The Emergence of the Second American Party System in Cumberland County, North Carolina.* Baton Rouge: Louisiana State University Press, 1981.

———. *Liberty and Power: The Politics of Jacksonian America.* New York: Hill and Wang, 1990.

Watts, Steven. *The Republic Reborn: War and the Making of Liberal America, 1790-1820.* Baltimore: Johns Hopkins University Press, 1987.

Wellman, Judith. *The Road to Seneca Falls: Elizabeth Cady Stanton and the First Woman's Rights Convention.* Urbana: University of Illinois Press, 2004.

Welter, Barbara. "The Cult of True Womanhood: 1820-1860." *American Quarterly* 18, no. 2 (1966): 151-74.

Wilburn, Jean Alexander. *Biddle's Bank: The Crucial Years.* New York: Columbia University Press, 1967.

Wilentz, Sean. *Andrew Jackson.* New York: Henry Holt, 2005.

———. *Chants Democratic: New York City and the Rise of the American Working Class, 1788-1850.* New York: Oxford University Press, 1984.

———. "On Class and Politics in Jacksonian America." *Reviews in American History* 10 (December 1982): 45-63.

———. *The Rise of American Democracy: Jefferson to Lincoln.* New York: W. W. Norton, 2005.

Wilson, Major. "Republicanism and the Idea of Party in the Jacksonian Period." *Journal of the Early Republic* 8 (1988): 419-42.

Wilson, Major L. *Space, Time and Freedom: The Quest for National Identity and the Irrepressible Conflict, 1815-1861.* Westport, Conn.: Greenwood Press, 1974.

Wood, Gordon S. *The Creation of the American Republic, 1776-1787.* Chapel

Hill: University of North Carolina Press, 1969. Paperback ed., New York: W. W. Norton, 1972.

Yee, Shirley J. *Black Women Abolitionists: A Study in Activism, 1828-1860.* Knoxville: University of Tennessee Press, 1992.

Yellin, Jean Fagan, and John C. Van Horne, eds. *The Abolitionist Sisterhood: Women's Political Culture in Antebellum America.* Ithaca, N.Y.: Cornell University Press, 1994.

Young, Mary E. *Redskins, Ruffleshirts and Rednecks: Indian Allotments in Alabama and Mississippi, 1830-1860.* Norman: University of Oklahoma Press, 1961.

Zaeske, Susan. *Signatures of Citizenship: Petitioning, Antislavery, and Women's Political Identity.* Chapel Hill: University of North Carolina Press, 2003.

Contributors

MARK R. CHEATHEM received his PhD from Mississippi State University in 2002 and is associate professor of history at Cumberland University in Lebanon, Tennessee. He is the author of *Old Hickory's Nephew: The Political and Private Struggles of Andrew Jackson Donelson* (2007) and editor of *Jacksonian and Antebellum Age: People and Perspectives* (2008). Currently he is working on a biography of Andrew Jackson that examines Old Hickory's southern identity.

JOHN T. ELLISOR serves as assistant professor of history at Columbus State University in Columbus, Georgia. He received his PhD from the University of Tennessee in 1996 and is the author of *The Second Creek War: Interethnic Conflict and Collusion on a Collapsing Frontier* (2010).

KEVIN M. GANNON received his PhD in 2002 at the University of South Carolina and currently serves as associate professor of history and codirector of the New Student Seminar Program at Grand View University in Des Moines, Iowa. He has written on states' rights and nullification movements in antebellum America for the *Journal of the Early Republic* and *Ohio History* and has presented his research on nullification, secession, and state formation theory at numerous conferences. He is currently completing a book manuscript titled *Riot and Rebellion in Early America*.

KRISTOFER RAY is assistant professor of early American history at Austin Peay State University and senior editor of the *Tennessee Historical Quarterly*. He received his PhD from the University of North Carolina at Chapel Hill in 2003. Between 2004 and 2006, he helped edit four volumes of *The Papers of Thomas Jefferson: Retirement Series*. His first book, *Middle Tennessee, 1775–1825: Progress and Popular Democracy on the Southwestern Frontier,* was published in 2007. He is currently researching issues of sovereignty, loyalty, and identity formation in the trans-Appalachian west, 1670–1800.

RYAN RUCKEL's scholarly interests include Andrew Jackson and the Jacksonian life of the mind, especially the role Providence played in the Jacksonian worldview. A veteran educator, he has taught in public schools, community colleges, and universities, including the Louisiana State University and Texas A&M University. Currently, he teaches history for one of the nation's oldest two-year institutions of higher learning, Pearl River Community College, in South Mississippi. He holds degrees from Trinity University (BA, 1988), the University of Southern Mississippi (MA, 1997), and the Louisiana State University (PhD, 2006).

BETH A. SALERNO is the author of *Sister Societies: Women's Antislavery Organizations in Antebellum America* (2005). She is associate professor of history and director of the Center for Teaching Excellence at Saint Anselm College in Manchester, New Hampshire. She received her PhD from the University of Minnesota-Twin Cities in 2000 and is currently working on a biography of New Hampshire abolitionist Mary Clark.

WADE SHAFFER is professor of history and associate provost of academic affairs at West Texas A&M University. He earned his PhD in American history from the College of William and Mary in 1993. His recent publications include "Beyond Franklin and Zenger: The Press in Colonial America," in the *Texas Journal of Genealogy and History,* and "Joseph William Chinn," in the *Dictionary of Virginia Biography.* He is currently working on a biography of Thomas Ritchie, the longtime editor of the *Richmond Enquirer.*

Index